KIDS
in
DANGER

KIDS IN DANGER

Disarming the Destructive Power of Anger in Your Child

Ross Campbell, MD
with Carole Sanderson Streeter

Chariot Victor Publishing
A Division of Cook Communications

Editor: Barbara Williams

Cover Design: Koechel Peterson & Associates

ISBN: 0-78143-391-6

1 2 3 4 5 6 7 8 9 10 Printing/Year 03 02 01 00 99

CONTENTS

Introduction

Dear Parents,

Since I first wrote this book in 1995, the effects of mishandled anger in our children and youth have tremendously increased. The most frightening and obvious examples are the school shootings in Kentucky, Arkansas, Oregon, Colorado, Georgia, Canada, and other places here and abroad. We also see the increase of disrespect for authority in our youth resulting in disillusionment in our teachers, youth ministers, and others who work with young people. Parents are of course the most affected by their child's failure to handle anger maturely.

I know that you are deeply concerned about the future of your children. So am I. And I know that you are wondering why it has become so difficult to understand the violence and other manifestations of anger in our society. This book deals with preventing these terrible results of anger in a child's life.

Why is all this tragedy happening? Because the appropriate ways of handling anger must be learned. They do not come naturally. And the mature management of anger must be taught in the home. Tragically, this is seldom done today. It is critical for all parents to know that *the primary lifetime threat to your child is his or her own anger.* However, if anger is handled well, it can actually be a positive force in your child's life. Your child must be *trained* to manage anger. In my opinion, this is the most difficult responsibility we parents have.

Anger is a little understood emotion—why we feel it, how we express it, and how we can change the way we deal with frustration. Unless we parents know what anger is and how to handle it in appropriate ways, we will not be able to teach our children what to do when they feel angry. Yes, *when*, for we all get angry every day.

In this book, we will be looking at some important definitions of anger, as well as at our own expressions of it. We will also talk about the various stages of our children's lives and the expressions of anger appropriate to each.

The challenge for all of us is to come to the point where we do not sin in our anger. That is a tall order, but one in which God will help us.

Ross Campbell, M.D.
Signal Mountain, Tennessee
1999

O N E

Your Child and Anger

It may surprise you that the primary lifetime threat to your child is his or her own anger. If it is not handled well, it will damage or destroy your child. The mishandling of anger is related to every present and potential problem your child may have — from poor grades to damaged relationships to possible suicide. It is imperative that you do all you can to safeguard your child now and in the future.

Violence is eating away at families and at society. We parents are the only ones who are empowered to teach our children how to handle their anger. And yet, in most homes this is not happening, and the majority of children are being taught how to handle anger in an inappropriate and immature manner. The reason for this is that most parents have been taught wrong ways of dealing with their own anger, and they pass along misguided ideas to their children.

Because children are basically powerless, they seek ways to control their world. As they grow older, they want to feel and appear autonomous. This desire for areas of control and the levels of independence is not bad in itself, but it needs to be exercised in appropriate ways for each age-level and station in life.

You want your children to learn respect for others and also for authority. This means that they must know how to handle conflict—not just over a toy now, but over contracts and relationships and sensitive issues later on. Because poor control of anger is a national epidemic, the only hope for your children is proper parenting. The way anger is managed in your home is the example they will probably follow. They will not see many demonstrations of good anger management in society or on television.

You also want your children to become people of integrity. This word is defined as "soundness, incorruptibility, completeness, honesty, unity." It means that a person is whole, all of one piece, acting with the same character qualities in one situation as in another.

The goal of this book is to help you raise your children to be people of integrity. The following definition of integrity is one that you should teach to your children as soon as they are old enough to understand it, and then teach it again and again as they grow older and the definition has larger meanings for their lives.

> A Person of Integrity Will Always . . .
> - tell the truth
> - keep his or her promises
> - take responsibility for personal behavior.

Poor management of anger and anti-authority attitudes are the enemies of integrity. The person who is rebelling against authority is tempted to lie, to break promises, and then to excuse bad behavior.

As this book was in process, the scandals of the young royals in England seemed to be at a peak. In a book written about Prince Charles, he was quoted as saying that he had taken his wedding vows with less than full intention to keep them. Following the release of the book, a member of the Anglican clergy appeared on television to question whether Charles should ever become King of England, since he had taken sacred vows dishonestly and possibly would do so again.

While your children will not take royal vows, the promises and commitments they make are just as important, and the way they conduct their lives will have impact not only on their peers, but also on succeeding generations.

WHY ARE PEOPLE SO ANGRY?

Why are children so angry? Why do they become angry adults? The most prevalent cause of anger in children is the feeling in their hearts that they are not loved enough. Children instinctively know that they need love, and they also know that it is their parents' responsibility to give them that feeling of love.

While most of them could not explain it very clearly, children know they cannot live happily or develop normally without the security of unconditional love. Yet, few of them feel genuinely loved and cared for by their parents.

Since children instinctively understand that parents are responsible to provide this gift of love, their natural response when it is withheld is anger. Of course, there are other causes of anger or rage in a child, but these are usually specific events such as disappointments, conflicts, abuse, fears, losses, and so on.

In the majority of homes, even in the best of homes,

the children do not *feel* loved. Many parents find this hard to understand, since they truly do love their children. How do we explain these opposing perceptions?

The reason is that few parents know how to transmit their heartfelt love to the heart of the child. Most parents are *verbally oriented* and they believe that telling a child, "I love you," communicates their love. While the verbal expression of love is important, it is far from sufficient.

Children are *behaviorally oriented*, which means that they must be loved on their terms. We will be talking about this more in future chapters, and you can find the subject dealt with at greater length in my books, *How to Really Love Your Child* and *How to Really Love Your Teenager*.

For now, let me say that when the child does not feel loved, he cannot grow to be his best, and as a result, he will feel continuing anger at his parents. This anger interferes with the child's basic development and later with adult behavior.

Perhaps an example will help you to see the difference between verbal and behavioral orientation. When my younger son, Dale, was five years old and I was out of town, I could call home and say to my wife, "I just wanted to tell you that I love you." That would make her the happiest gal in Tennessee.

But if I got Dale on the phone and said, "I just wanted to tell you that I love you," he would likely respond, "Sure, Daddy, but why did you call?"

The verbal expression of love was meaningful to Pat, but it didn't have very deep significance for Dale. Being a child, he was behaviorally oriented. To convey the message of love from my heart to his meant doing something behavioral when I returned home.

ANGER AND POWERLESSNESS

In his book *Make Anger Your Ally,* Neil Clark Warren offers some definitions and causes of anger that we need to look at and then apply to children:

> The capacity to become angry is an impressive gift which comes as part of our biological inheritance.
>
> Anger is a physical state of readiness. When we are angry, we are prepared to act. . . .
>
> The whole purpose of anger is to give us the wherewithal for managing our environment — particularly those parts which cause us to feel hurt, frustrated, or fearful. If we do that poorly, we will regularly experience a sense of inadequacy and helplessness.[1]

As you read this, did you apply it to yourself? If so, you will want to read it again, thinking about your children, and also about those children whose experiences cause them to regularly feel hurt, frustrated, and fearful.

Think too about children in good homes where certain events and emotions are well beyond their capacity to understand or interpret correctly.

Dr. Warren makes another observation that is worth our consideration in this regard — that the most important factor in handling anger is to get our self-concept into shape. "When it comes to taking charge of your life, literally nothing is as important as a solidly constructed self-system." The main reason for this is that "when your self-concept is well put together and you have a plentiful supply of self-esteem, you have ample energy to run your life."[2] Also, fewer things will make you feel angry.

Like all of us, children become angry when they perceive a situation or person as frustrating, threatening, or hurtful.

But, unlike adults, children do not have the power to make radical changes in their lives. They have a weak power base, little autonomy, and only occasional independence.

And, unlike most adults, children do not have a self-system in place. They live with parents or other adults who are there to help them in the formation of a self-system and self-concept. Yes, many children do possess a remarkably well-formed self-concept for their age. What they lack is the knowledge and experience to interpret the world in relation to themselves.

The formation of children is within the care of their parents. To deliberately threaten, hurt, or frustrate these children is something like putting on your hiking boots and then walking through the beautiful flower garden your neighbor has spent months cultivating, destroying the blossoms as you go. But deliberately causing harm to children is far more serious than this, because we are dealing with human souls, with God-given potential, with eternal consequences.

You may want to think about the dynamics in your home, and possible ways you might be causing or allowing hurt or frustration to your children, even unintentionally.

Put yourself in the place of each child and ask how you might react to specific situations and attitudes.

EXPRESSIONS OF ANGER

When we are faced with a threatening situation, why do we express anger? We do so to "manage those internal and external sources of hurt, frustration, and threat" and keep "inner pain to an absolute minimum."[3]

Children and adults don't express anger all that differently. Yes, adults use a larger vocabulary and have a wider variety of resources to draw from, including physical strength, but it is uncanny to watch an angry adult through squinted eyes and to imagine that you are seeing an eight-year-old. There often isn't that much difference.

When adults express anger, they do it from a power base. When children express anger, they do it from a dependent state, as well as from their immature understandings. They are clever at using all the leverage they can manage, but it still isn't enough to effect the changes they want.

When you feel angry, you usually—but not always—know what is wrong and what you wish would change. When a child is angry, he or she sometimes knows what is the matter, but probably not as often as you do. For this reason, you need to ask, "What is bothering this child? What does he want? Is it possible? Is it reasonable? Did someone else cause the distress or frustration?"

What the child wants often is neither reasonable nor possible. He may just wish he were older or bigger, or had more power or space or money. He may be responding to growth cycles or hormones. He may have been treated unfairly by people none of you can control. He may wish he had some of the advantages his friends enjoy.

If, however, you know what caused the hurt or frustration, and if—God forbid—you are the one who did it, make tracks to correct the situation. Growing up is hard enough as it is, without people we love making it more difficult.

SIX ANGRY CHILDREN

Teaching a child how to handle anger is the most difficult part of parenting. Because it is sometimes hard to recognize demonstrations of anger in our children, I want us to look at six children, ranging in age from four to sixteen, to see how they are showing their anger.

♦ Four-year-old Janie was potty-trained when she was eighteen months old. For the past six months, however, she has been soiling her pants. Her parents have talked to their doctor and have tried everything they can think of. There is no physical problem, and yet Janie continues this behavior.

♦ Eight-year-old John continually picks on his younger brother and sister, often hurting them. His parents don't know how to stop this behavior, and they worry about John.

♦ Nine-year-old Joey gave his parents no unusual problems until the middle of the school year, when his teacher sent home a note saying that Joey had not been turning in his homework. His grades were going down, and this became a matter of concern for both teacher and parents.

♦ Thirteen-year-old Debbie has always been vivacious and outgoing. Now she is withdrawing from her parents and is very difficult to talk to. She acts sullen and spends much time in her room alone. Her parents don't know if this is part of early adolescence or if they should be concerned.

♦ Fifteen-year-old Jessica was always a delight to her parents and teachers, as well as to her friends. You can imagine how shocked her parents were when they found marijuana paraphernalia in her room. When they took her to the doctor, they also discovered that she was pregnant.

♦ Sixteen-year-old Ken did well in school until last year when his grades began to fall. Now there is danger of his failing the semester. Ken is a bright boy with no learning disabilities, and is capable of doing fine work in school. He still has a good attitude and wants to do well, so that he can be accepted at a competitive university.

What is happening in the lives of all these children? As I counseled with them and their parents, I discovered that each one was acting out anger, either consciously or unconsciously. None of these children was being trained to handle anger properly, because the parents didn't understand how important this is.

I am not blaming the parents as I say this, because most parents believe that anger is always bad and should be "disciplined out of the child." As a result, the parents respond in confusing ways when a child becomes angry.

That parents are confused about anger is not surprising, since many professionals are also. Anger is very difficult to understand. After studying it for twenty-five years, I still am not sure about some aspects of it.

However, I do know how crucial it is for parents to train their children how to properly express their anger. One caution—you can never do this with a how-to manual.

SIX CHILDREN IN NEED

It is time to return to our six children and try to determine what each one was saying through the expressions of anger.

♦ Janie was indeed expressing anger as she soiled her pants. Because this is generally not recognized as a sign of anger, it is usually treated by physical means alone, and the anger which is causing the behavior is left to grow and cause even worse problems for the child later on. This is a classic example of passive-aggressive behavior, a subconscious expression of anger. We will talk about this in chapter 6.

♦ John's belligerence and violence toward his brother and sister was creating chaos for the entire family. This type of situation is difficult to correct, because the behaviors become entrenched in all the family members and get worse. Until John's aggression was identified as an outworking of anger, no progress could be made.

Aggression is one of the common immature expressions of anger. Passive aggression was also adding to this situation, making it even worse.

♦ Joey's "forgetting" to turn in his work is a classic sign of anger which often begins around age nine or ten. It is another example of subconsciously motivated passive aggression.

♦ Debbie's radical change in behavior was an indication of teenage depression. But it was the anger component of the depression that was so destructive and so out of proportion to the other factors in Debbie's case. If nothing had been done for her, she would have faced a bleak future.

Teenage depression is a special and often dangerous source of anger that needs to be understood by parents. As we will see later, passive-aggressive behavior is to some extent normal in the early adolescent child. But in Debbie's case, it had been maximized to dangerous proportion by her depression. If you would like to receive a pamphlet about teenage depression, you can write to me in care of Victor Books.

♦ Jessica's situation is all too common today. Her drug use and her pregnancy were signs of desperation. We can wonder why her deep needs came out in such heartbreaking ways.

Jessica's poor means of handling her anger began years ago and her parents suspected that something was wrong. And yet, her many strengths and winning ways convinced them that she was all right. Her parents did the best they could do, but their best was complicated by the fact that they had never learned to manage their own anger well. And, of course, they didn't know that one of their most critical responsibilities as parents was to train their children to manage anger.

♦ Ken's falling grades were due to teenage depression and the resulting passive-aggressive behavior which usually accompanies depression. As you read on, you will better understand how the various immature ways of handling anger cause so many childhood and adolescent problems. It is particularly crucial that you understand passive-aggressive behavior, since it can intensify existing difficulties.

LOOKING AHEAD

As you think toward your children's future, you may have never considered what their anger will do. It is always easier to worry about what someone else's anger might do.

As I said at the beginning of this chapter, the primary lifetime threat to your child is his or her own anger. It can harm your child in every way, and is related to all other problems he or she may have.

With the devastating situations in our world, it is essential that we as parents do all we can to safeguard the future of our dear children.

Since few parents manage their own anger well, most children are not being taught how to handle their anger. As a result, our society is falling victim to this growing destruction.

If you want your children to be able to express anger in mature ways, you will need to make sure you know how to do this also. In chapter 8, we will be discussing the self-knowledge that parents need in order to be able to train their children.

I am a fortunate father. When my children were young, I did not know how to train them in handling anger. But I learned these vital lessons early enough so that my wife and I could train them when they were small. Our goal was to have them reach a significant level of maturity by the time they were seventeen, so that we and they could feel confident of their passage into the adult world.

Carey, David, and Dale are now adults who are managing their anger well, sometimes better than I do. As I observe them, one of my greatest joys in life is to see them functioning as morally and ethically strong people.

I am also profoundly thankful that my children are free of the typical emotional scars and pain that so many children carry into adult life. I refer especially to that sense of deprivation, that nagging sense that something vital is missing from their lives. It is this which prevents many adults from being and doing all that they would like to be and do. This feeling of deprivation comes not only from a lack of unconditional love, but also from the mishandling of anger.

Two of the greatest gifts you can give your children are to love them unconditionally and to teach them to manage their anger in ever more mature ways.

T W O

Society and Anger

I am astounded at the change in perception of children in our country over the past several decades. Until recently, children were accepted as innocent, endearing, and lovable by almost everyone. But over time, this has changed.

Today, growing numbers of people consider children to be annoyances, hindrances, and often undesirable. Even worse, some are depicting children as creatures with evil intent.

So much anger today is expressed against children, either in outright violence or in passive ways, that it is easy to wonder how many people in America really like children. Consider what is happening:

♦ Children's needs are generally given low priority. Even hardened criminals receive better services than many of our children. It is not that public officials are unaware of the needs of children. They even push state lotteries to finance education. But after millions of dollars have been collected, the funds for schools often don't increase.

♦ Many schools have become places of chaos instead of orderly refuges where children can learn. The Centers for Disease Control in Atlanta have listed school violence as a public-health concern in the United States.

♦ The media has moved in deliberate war against teenagers and children, sending degenerate "entertainment" into our homes.

♦ Advertisers exploit the weaknesses and desires of the young.

♦ Crime is rampant, and often its victims are children. The weapon of choice may be hands, guns, knives, or cars. Some people are so twisted that they mourn the death of murderers more than they mourn the victims.

♦ We have become a nation of victims, with millions of people blaming others for their own antisocial behavior.

Children grow up so fast. Today, they hardly have time to catch their breath before they are launched into an aggressive and permissive adult world.

No longer are they seen as the meaning of our lives, our hope for the future, our heart-warmers, the ones who keep us going. As society concentrates more and more on adult desires, children are the losers.

We parents who care deeply about our children have been pushed into a cruel place in society. We love our children, and want what is best for them. Yet, beyond our own efforts, we often feel helpless in a world that is so alien to our Judeo-Christian values. It is easy to be angry at the powers that be, at the named and unnamed forces in society that make this world an unfriendly and difficult place for families.

As a recent article in *Reader's Digest* said, "The bar-

barians are not at the gates. They are inside. The question of the hour—and of the next century—is whether all this can be turned around."[1]

If anyone is to make a difference in society for children, it will have to be parents—those of us who care, who band together to say, "Enough is enough!"

WHERE DO CHILDREN FIND LOVE?

Children receive love and personal identity from three sources. It is in these places that they find out who they are and how they are to think about life.

♦ Home and family. This includes the extended family, those who also love our children and make room for them in their homes and hearts.

♦ Community. This reaches to school, neighborhoods, work, clubs, sports, and social pursuits.

♦ Church. This is where they learn of God's love for them and discover their identity as part of the people of God. In church children should also feel a part of the supportive fellowship that is to characterize the body of Christ.

The sad fact today is that many children are growing up with only two, or one, or even none of these sources of love and identity functioning for them.

The adults in these children's lives may have never experienced adequate love when they were young, or perhaps they are too busy with their own schedules, and the children are left to fend for themselves. Some of them fend with every material benefit, but they still can't manufacture unconditional love and a satisfying sense of identity.

REBELLION AGAINST AUTHORITY

Because so many people are starved for love, they are angry and they show their anger in rebellion. Where does this anti-authority attitude come from?

Anti-authority attitudes are formed in childhood. They are an expression of subconscious anger that comes from children not being taught to express their anger in appropriate ways and, ultimately, from not feeling sufficiently loved. This subconscious anger has contributed to the decline of authority in our public life.

By *authority* I mean the legal and moral forces that enable us to live in an orderly society, with a reasonable chance for security and safety. For many people today, this chance does not exist, and fear is epidemic among Americans, fear for themselves and for their children.

A primary cause for this fear is the rebellion of others against valid authority. Where does such rebellion come from?

At the risk of sounding simplistic, I want to suggest a simple answer.

♦ Rebellion against authority comes from anger.

♦ Anger comes from not feeling adequately loved.

♦ A lack of love in the lives of children comes from adults who don't know how to show love—or don't care to.

Many years ago, Robert Nisbet wrote *The Decline of Authority*, a book that stimulated much discussion. At that time the problem seemed more academic than actual. But more than he ever predicted has come to being.

Dr. Benjamin Spock, famed baby doctor, describes himself as "in despair" over the condition of our society today. In his book *A Better World for Our Children*, he says that he is deeply saddened by the "brutal state of our neighborhoods where our children now dodge bullets instead of playing dodge ball," and where children must deal with divorce and violence in their daily lives. Dr. Spock believes that the deterioration in America has been caused by a fundamental loss of values.[2]

But this loss of values is a demonstration of the anti-authority attitude so prevalent in society today. When a child does not learn to handle anger appropriately, this misguided anger will manifest itself in childhood and later in adult life against parents, laws, and all types of values, including the spiritual.

We just need to pick up a newspaper or watch the news to be convinced of the anti-authority attitudes so rampant in the world. Or, look at MTV, if you can stand it, or the many ads that are on the edge of rebellion.

Morality in this country has reached an all-time low in the last twenty-five years. In this short span, we have heard educators tell teens that their bodies are their own, and that they can do with them what they want, including any kind of sexual activity or abortion.

The language and actions common in "family entertainment" used to be prohibited on stage and screen.

And crime? Well, just look at the cases that were in the news during the months this book was in preparation.

♦ The O.J. Simpson murder trial

♦ The Menendez brothers' murder trial

♦ Chicago children who killed children

♦ The Smith toddlers drowned by their mother

These are the sensational cases. But every day the local news is filled with the same kinds of rebellions by people who never learned how to handle their anger.

Rebellion against authority also affects the church as people want a more individualized expression of their "faith" that may or may not express the historic doctrines of the Christian church. This is evident from the numbers of people who say they believe in God and in Jesus, but who do not have a vital relationship with Jesus Christ as their Lord and Savior. It is also evident in church fights that end up in hostility or in church splits.

TAKING RESPONSIBILITY

Integrity is in short supply in society, and nowhere is this more evident than on the political scene which has become a picture of unkept pledges and disregard of the public. Basic trustworthiness, where a person's word "is as good as gold" seems to be a thing of the past among public persons.

But it isn't only the politicians who are at fault. When did you last hear someone take full responsibility for his or her actions? Taking responsibility means facing the fact that we may be wrong, in opinion or behavior. It means constantly evaluating our behavior and being willing to correct it when we need to. If we fail to do this, we end up blaming others.

I just read of a classic case of blame. A dentist who had molested some of his female patients lost his license. His response was to sue his insurance company for disability pay to the tune of a million dollars. How did he justify this? He claimed that his behavior resulted from "mental illness."

We need a return to the quality of integrity expressed by General Eisenhower during World War II. Before the invasion, he prepared a press release, in case the invasion failed. It said, in part, "If any blame or fault attaches to the attempt, it is mine alone."

SIGNS OF HOPE

Not all public demonstrations of anger are violent or inappropriate. Just think of MADD, Mothers Against Drunk Driving, which was started by mothers who lost children to drunk drivers. Of course, they were angry, but they chose to channel their anger into a crusade against public toleration of those who drive while intoxicated.

A spinoff of MADD is SADD, Students Against Drunk Driving, an organization that meets in many schools, to educate and also harness young energies against this plague that affects so many teenagers.

Most of us remember Martin Luther King's peaceful marches against discrimination. The fact that they were nonviolent made them all the more powerful.

In 1982, Deborah Larbalestrier, an older woman living in Los Angeles became a household name on the West Coast because of her courageous use of her anger. Living in a crime-ridden section of the city, she felt helpless to stop what was happening all around her. But then, one day she saw two boys trying to steal her neighbor's car. They knew she was watching and the whole scene outraged her. As the story was reported in the *Los Angeles Times*:

> I went out there with a stick and I told them, "How dare you insult me that way, robbing this car right in my face as if I didn't exist?"
>
> The teenagers ran off, but Larbalestrier wanted to make sure they didn't return. So she called a meeting on her block and told them, "We've become prisoners in our own homes. . . . We have to take our neighborhood back."
>
> Then Larbalestrier went to the Los Angeles Police Department's Wilshire Division to organize a Neighborhood Watch club for her street.[3]

At the time the article was written, the neighborhood had been crime-free for eighteen months.

CHILDREN AND HOPE FOR SOCIETY

Every society reflects what its children know. Yesterday's children are today's adults, and the children in your home will soon be grown. There is hope for our society if enough people learn how to use their anger appropriately and constructively. Anger does not have to lead to violence. It does not need to get out of control. Anger is a gift we can learn to use in beneficial ways.

There is hope for society if parents will become more intentional about teaching their children how to manage anger. For many parents, this will first mean learning to understand and manage their own anger in better ways.

It will also include teaching children to respect authority, even when they don't agree with what is happening.

Children need to learn from example and from history that there are more acceptable ways to disagree than violent behavior.

If you feel that your children are doing well in their expressions of anger, you can't avoid the fact that many others are not. At least one third of adolescents are subjected to abusive relationships. Children are committing unprecedented cruelty and violence. Teenagers are 7 percent of the population and commit 17 percent of violent crimes.

Above all, you do not want your children to become part of those statistics, or to become victims of others who have not learned to control their anger. You want them to grow into adults of unquestioned integrity.

If your family is doing well, you may want to reach out to children and families who are in need of help. For there is hope only as we work together. The problem is too big for any one of us; but all of us together *can* make a difference.

THREE

Your Home and Anger

Wouldn't it be wonderful if all the anger in society could be left outside the doors of our homes? If what happened inside our homes was in contrast to what all the members of the family faced every day at work, school, and in the community?

As wonderful as that would be, it won't happen, because we are carriers. Rather like carriers of disease, we carry anger and frustration with us. We bring stress and tension and tiredness home with us, and then we each play off the tensions and angers of others in the house.

If we are sensitive enough to realize what is happening and to change course, we can go a long way toward altering the script. But if we don't do this, chaos can result. And children are the victims — in two ways. First, they have to live with the unmanaged anger of adults. And second, they don't learn how to deal with their own anger.

You know of the Centers for Disease Control in Atlanta. Maybe we need Centers for Anger Control, and not just in one place. Every home could be such a center, where anger is diagnosed and then managed to the benefit of all. If this is what you want for your home, you can make it happen.

THE ATMOSPHERE OF YOUR HOME

One of the most powerful influences on a child's self-esteem and self-concept is the atmosphere of the home. When I enter a home, I can quickly tell whether a child will thrive there. Each home has its own atmosphere, and some qualities of this are fairly neutral, like colors and styles, while other qualities tend to be more positive or negative.

The atmosphere in one home may be warm, relaxed, calm, friendly, accepting, and upbeat. People feel comfortable in such a home, and a child living there can grow to be her best. She can relax in the support and encouragement that the parents provide, and can use her energies to develop in every part of her life.

However, few children are blessed with such a setting. Instead, they live in homes that are tense, judgmental, pessimistic, and rejecting. When children live in this type of environment, they have to use most of their energy trying to cope with the lack of love and support. Because it is more difficult for them to develop normally, they probably will feel angry at their parents. Also, they will likely not learn to handle their own anger in a mature way.

As parents, you need to remember that you control the atmosphere in which your children grow. They are powerless and have to depend on you to provide what they need.

I know that you want to feel good about the kind of job you are doing as parents. You are making a major investment of love and care and money and time in your family and you want this investment to turn out well, not just for you but for your children. You care deeply about them and want them to have happy and successful lives.

When children are small, it is so easy to feel hopeful

about them. They are innocent and manageable and dependent. But as they grow older, many parents feel discouraged and disappointed about what is happening in their families. One of the key causes for this is unmanaged anger.

Without an understanding of childhood anger and how they can deal with it, parents are likely to feel like failures, in spite of all the things they know they are doing right. Many children have an anti-parent attitude because they don't feel loved, and they can express this attitude in horrifying ways. Consider the stories of Ann and Todd.

ANN

A smartly dressed couple entered my office. I saw in my appointment book that they were Jim and Mary Perkins. The notation beneath their names said that their fifteen-year-old daughter, Ann, was pregnant.

As they sat down, I realized that Mary looked familiar. "We've met somewhere, haven't we?" I asked.

She managed a tight smile. "I've shown you a table several times at the Sailmaker Restaurant."

"You're the hostess at lunchtime. I was there last Tuesday."

I turned to Jim, and asked about his work. "I'm an accountant," he replied.

"That figures," I punned, trying to lighten the air.

We spent a few minutes more on small talk and discovered that we had mutual friends at their church.

With a glance at my appointment book, I turned to Mary and said, "You came to talk about Ann. Tell me about her."

Tears welled up in Mary's eyes. "Dr. Campbell, she's only fifteen, just a year out of middle school. The youngest of our four. And she's pregnant! What are we going to do?"

The words were gushing out as she kept dabbing her eyes. "We did everything we knew to be good parents to Ann. We've both worked for years to give her and the others the good things in life. We took them all to Sunday School and church. We gave Ann piano lessons and sent her to music camp for several years. She is so talented and beautiful. How are we ever going to handle this?" And Mary's voice trailed off in sobs.

Jim twisted in his chair and then began. "I just don't know where we went wrong. Why did she get herself into this mess? Why has she become so defiant? She's against everything Mary and I try to do for her."

As I talked with Mary and Jim, I realized that they truly loved Ann, but too often communicated that love by giving her things and advantages. They honestly felt that this would make up for not spending time with her.

When I met with Ann, my suspicions were confirmed. She did not feel that her parents loved her or that she was important to them.

Defiantly she said, "I don't know why I got pregnant. I just did. I could have prevented it—I know how. Maybe I wanted to be somebody too, like my mother. If I became a mother, then I would be important. *Someone* would love *me*."

For several weeks, I met with the Perkins family. At first, Ann was reserved and expressed few feelings, but I could see that she was angry and frustrated. After several sessions, she began to open up.

"Remember the night of the mother-daughter banquet, Mom? You couldn't be there because you had to go with Daddy to that accountants' seminar. I was the only one there without a mother!"

"But Ann," Mary interrupted, "we talked about that and I bought you a lovely dress for the banquet. I thought you didn't mind that I went with Daddy."

"Well, I did mind! You guys never seem to be around when I need you. My friends' parents always drive us to games and stuff; you never offer to drive. I'm always bumming rides with someone else."

"Now wait a minute, Ann," her father jumped in. "You're talking like we never do anything for you. I happen to know that you are quite an accomplished pianist. Who took you to all those lessons? And who paid for them?"

"Big deal, Daddy! Anyway, how would you know whether I can play the piano? The last time you attended one of my recitals was when I was ten!"

During outbursts like these, Jim would often leave the room. But over the next weeks, he and Mary began to understand Ann's feelings. They realized that the things they had given her could not begin to replace the personal attention she needed from them. They had left Ann with an empty emotional tank.

As we continued to talk, Jim and Mary worked hard to gain insights into Ann's problems and to find ways to share in her life. As Ann heard her parents express their love and concern for her, and as she experienced it daily at home, she began to communicate with them in a more positive way.

It was a slow and painful process, but Ann and her parents began to really get acquainted with each other. A key to their success was their desire to have a loving family. As Ann felt her parents' love, her anger began to subside. Their love, and the feelings of self-worth that Ann experienced, went a long way toward sustaining her in the difficult months that followed.

TODD

Mark Johnson sat across from me, impatiently tapping his well-manicured fingers on the arm of the chair. His appearance suggested affluence. His wife, Brenda, whose attire was equally perfect, was also impatient.

The Johnsons were active in a large church, and all indications gave them the mark of being a successful couple in more ways than financial. Their daughter, Amy, was six and their son, Todd, was eleven. I wasn't sure why they were in my office.

Brenda began, "Dr. Campbell, we need to talk with you about Todd. Six months ago, he seemed to change from a normal boy into a quiet stranger who is angry all the time. He constantly finds excuses to stay away from us. Goodness knows, we have little enough time to spend with each other. Mark's law practice is growing, and my children's shop keeps me there many evenings."

"Yes, Dr. Campbell," Mark agreed, "and you'd think the kids would appreciate all that we can do for them because we work such long hours. Amy hasn't given us any trouble, but Todd is a different story. A few nights ago, some of his older friends brought him home drunk. What in the world would make an eleven-year-old kid who has everything do such a thing?"

"We're shocked beyond words," added Brenda. "And to make matters worse, Todd has disrupted the entire household with this silly stunt. Mark had to reschedule his clients, and I am taking time away from the store for this appointment. Don't get me wrong—we want to help Todd, but we don't understand why this has happened. As Mark said, we've given him everything, and this is the way he thanks us!"

As Mark paced my office floor, he asked, "What in the world is wrong with our boy? Or, could it be us? I can settle legal matters for the most important people in this city, but I can't make my own son happy."

What indeed would make an eleven-year-old use alcohol? For as we talked further, it came out that Todd had been drinking regularly but had been able to conceal it from his parents until now.

Todd was not alone in this behavior. Studies show that an increasing number of young teens and preteens are using alcohol and drugs. Many of them are from Christian families.

In Todd's case, as in so many others, the answer was in the deterioration of family life. His parents were too busy to make special time for him. As a result, he and Amy were receiving little nurture from the very people who were supposed to be giving it. This lack of time and nurture resulted in Todd having a very empty emotional tank. He did not feel loved. This made him angry and also put him in a position of vulnerability to peer pressure, to gain attention and acceptance.

MAKING TIME FOR FAMILY LIFE

Mark and Brenda Johnson are prime examples of parents who look perfect, but who put something else in place of family. In this instance, it was career. As a result, they had two lovely but unhappy children. Yes, we discovered that six-year-old Amy was also angry at her parents.

Both the Johnsons and the Perkins thought their children should just know that they were loved. But children don't "just know." They can't. All they know is how they feel, and both Ann and Todd felt unloved. Their feelings were based on the amount of time and emotional energy their parents invested in them.

Many parents today live with far too much stress and they just don't have the resiliency to deal calmly with normal childhood behaviors. I realize that it takes a lot out of parents to keep family and career and other obligations in good shape, especially when both of them are working. Many parents don't have the energy or perseverance or desire to do all that is required. Therefore, when something slips, it is almost always the quality of family life.

I want to say a word here about single-parent families, since some people believe that parents alone just can't do an adequate job of parenting. I have seen countless single parents give loving nurture and discipline to their children.

The key to a successful family is not whether it has two parents, but whether the parental focus is in the right place. A single parent can raise a child well and guide him through the "terrible teens" into responsible Christian adulthood, just as two parents can.

QUALITY TIME OR TIME?

We often hear about *quality time.* What really matters is TIME. Spending time with your family—getting to know your children, telling them that you love them, and letting them know they are important to you—these are the important things.

Commitment to the Christian family is based on the notion that we love one another, that we care about the emotional, physical, psychological, and spiritual needs of all family members.

If we love each other, we will want to be together for more than covering the necessities. We will want to enjoy the others in the family. It doesn't really matter what we do, just so long as we are having a loving and happy time together. As parents, we want our children to know that they are more important than the many influences that tend to separate parents and children.

The loving times shared by a family add to the strength of the individuals and also of the family as a unit. We make memories together as we spend leisure time in play or rest or travel or reading or whatever we like to do.

Think of your own happy memories from childhood. Are they more about presents and privileges or about gifts of love or time? What gives you warmer memories—the gifts you received or the feelings of closeness with your parents?

As I counseled with both the Johnsons and Perkins, they discovered that they were able to find time for family. The very fact that they could make time for the counseling sessions told them that. By carving out periods of time to enjoy one another, they were going a long way toward preventing further problems in the future.

It takes time to correct established patterns and form new ones, but these families are determined to make life better in the future.

FAMILY COMMUNICATION

In your communication with your children, you want to be personal to them. Family life should not look and sound like communication in any organization you are a part of. As parents we should be reaching in love for the personhood of our children.

Aaron, who took part in a survey of 1,055 teenagers said, "Even when my parents are here, it's like they're not, because they don't have any time." Although Aaron eats dinner with his parents, he said, "We never talk about anything. Maybe school. A lot of times they're paranoid about my friends. They always get on my case when I come home."[1]

One type of family communication which has received a lot of attention in recent years, particularly in certain religious circles, is the chain-of-command approach. If you have been in a military or business or family organization where this kind of communication is strictly followed, you know how depersonalizing it can be. For some reason, many religious leaders have advocated a chain-of-command approach to family life. What this actually means is that the father is the only really responsible person in the home. Anyone down the chain is responsible to do only what he or she is told, and this includes the wife and mother!

I realize that not everyone carries it to such an extreme, but I also know the devastating results in many families who have adopted this philosophy.

I think the approach began to strengthen in the 1960s, when people were alarmed at increased permissiveness and at the rebellious demonstrations against the Vietnam War. Certain "experts" were trained in behavior modification which is based on experimentation with rats. Failing to understand normal adolescent behavior and counterculture dynamics, these "experts" blamed parental permissiveness for most of the nation's problems. A subtle but fundamental change in parenting and parent-child relationships began to take place.

The change was from a cooperative and mutually supportive bond to a hierarchical chain-of-command based on discipline. In the first type, both the child and the parents assumed responsibility for the child's behavior. In the second, the parents assumed more responsibility for the child's behavior and the child less.

We are now trying to cope with a generation of children who refuse to take responsibility for their behavior and also refuse to learn how to do so.

Such miscommunication results in distrust, resentment, and lack of close-knit affection. This becomes a vicious cycle, for the more problems our young people experience, the more emphasis is placed on "discipline." The stricter the "discipline" without love and support, the angrier are the youth. As they have more problems with anger, the more anti-authority they become, and this translates into being antiparent, antimorality, anti-other people, antichurch, antilaw, and so on. We now have more than one generation of such people.

Some educators have suggested an answer to the inner needs of these children—to try to make them "feel good" through self-esteem techniques. Therefore, a child may receive special commendation for behaving in a pleasant and cooperative manner, something that should be expected, not rewarded.

In 1993, we were transfixed by a horrifying display of youthful rebellion, as the Menendez brothers were on trial for murdering their parents. Writing in *National Review*, Stuart Goldman suggests that the Menendez murders and the trial are an example of the self-esteem philosophy gone awry:

> In the cosmology of the self-help movement all human failure stems from our lack of ability to love ourselves; the worst thing a person can have is a bad case of low self-esteem. . . . In a world where morality is dictated by therapists rather than God, where evil is discounted as a myth, where feeling good is the end-all and be-all, they can be comforted by the thought that murdering an "abusive" parent is not only permissible—it is healthy.[2]

In later chapters we will talk more about specific communication with angry children. For now, though, I want to stress the importance of personal and loving interaction with your children. It is in this way that you will be able to teach them respect for other people and for themselves, and also help them to increasingly take responsibility for their behavior.

Such responsibility includes relationships with siblings in your family. If you treat each child with respect and firm love, and give proper guidance, you should be able to minimize conflict between brothers and sisters. In the Bible, God's children are told to love one another. Surely, the children in a family should do as much.

THE IMPORTANCE OF EXTENDED FAMILY

Because of time and career pressures, most parents feel the need of some relief and help with their children. I would like to suggest that grandparents and other extended family members consider taking a more active role in the lives of their young relatives.

Many grandparents today opt out of active participation with their grandchildren. While they may think that they are gaining independence and freedom, in the long run, they are losing years of loving interaction that can never be replaced.

Many nuclear families live with constant stress because they are far from relatives and have little or no support from close friends. I believe they need to ask themselves if this is really how they want to live. Their constant tension, and at times fear, is communicating all the wrong messages to the children.

I realize that solutions to this are not easy. Family members the same age as the parents probably have their own share of stresses. And some grandparents just don't want to be involved very much with their grandchildren. They seem to be saying, "I raised my family. Now you raise yours."

However, there may be some answers. If family members do want to be closer, someone may decide to make a geographical move to foster more involvement in extended family.

If this is impossible, the next best thing is to find some friends who can feel like family, and with whom you can build a small community of trust and mutual helpfulness. These may be people in your neighborhood or church, people close enough to you that they can know you and your children well and offer the kinds of support that family members would give, if they were just down the road, as aunts and uncles and grandparents used to be in another generation.

Making such arrangements for extended family, either actual relatives or close friends, will take some planning and may involve major changes. But after you decide what you most want for your family, and who can best contribute the gifts of time and love to your children, the sacrifices may be well worth the cost.

Trying to stretch yourselves beyond your resources will inevitably take a toll on you and your family. One result will probably be increased impatience and anger with your children.

Because children have no defense against parental anger, their hurt and frustration goes down deep inside and festers. To have one or more adults nearby who can love and care for your child will give you relief, and will also soothe your child's feelings, especially if you succumb to the pressures and express anger that you later regret.

AN ATMOSPHERE OF LOVE

Early in this chapter, we talked about the atmosphere of the home and the impact it has on the growing child. This familiar poem by Doris Law Nolte expresses so well the influence that the home environment has on a child.

Children Learn What They Live

If a child lives with criticism,
he learns to condemn.
If a child lives with hostility
he learns to fight.
If a child lives with ridicule,
he learns to be shy.
If a child lives with shame,
he learns to feel guilty.

If a child lives with tolerance,
he learns to be patient.
If a child lives with encouragement,
he learns confidence.
If a child lives with praise,
he learns to appreciate.
If a child lives with fairness,
he learns justice.
If a child lives with security,
he learns to have faith.
If a child lives with approval,
he learns to like himself.
If a child lives with acceptance and friendship,
he learns to find love in the world.

FOUR

Your Child's Need for Unconditional Love

Although they don't say it in so many words, the question our children are asking us all the time is, "Do you love me?" If we only *say*, "We love you," they are not going to receive the answer they need. The reason for this is that growing children are more *behaviorally oriented*, while adults are more *verbally oriented*. This means that we respond to words much more than children do. They need demonstrations of our love to really believe that we care.

Even in their unacceptable behaviors, including acting out their anger, children are asking, "Do you love me? Do you love me enough not to give up on me?" Because they are immature, children express anger immaturely, with ventilation and aggression. Therefore, this is what we must work with as we guide them into more mature expressions of anger. This means accepting their ways of expressing anger, not as desirable but as normal, if we hope to lead them away from these childish ways.

When our children are very young, we don't have a problem accepting other behaviors appropriate to each age. But many parents do have difficulty dealing with anger. And then in their feelings of frustration, they often fail to give unconditional love and acceptance to their children at the very time they most need it. In fact, the parents may anger them even more, because they treat them harshly.

When my children were younger, I had to frequently remind myself of several facts that should be obvious:

♦ Because they are children, they will act like children.

♦ Much childish behavior is unpleasant.

♦ If I do my part as a parent and love them despite their childish behavior, they will be able to give up their childish ways.

♦ If I love them only when they please me and convey my love only at these times (conditional love), they will not feel genuinely loved. This will make them feel insecure, and will prevent them from moving on to more self-control. Therefore, their behavior and development is my responsibility as much as theirs.

♦ If I love them unconditionally, they will feel good about themselves and be comfortable with themselves. They will then learn to control their anxiety and also their behavior.

♦ If I love them only when they meet my requirements or expectations, they will feel incompetent. They will believe it is useless to do their best, because it will never be enough. They will be plagued by insecurity, anxiety, and low self-esteem. Therefore, their total growth is as much my responsibility as theirs.[1]

CHILDREN NEED UNCONDITIONAL LOVE

Children are like mirrors. They reflect love much more than they initiate it. If love is given to them, they return it. If none is given, they have little or none to offer.

As your children are reaching for wholeness and for the completeness of character and experience you want them to have, they find their way by seeing reflections. They come to know themselves by looking in the mirror of your love. Some mirrors give a clear and full reflection, while others are cracked or marred.

When parental love is unconditional and constant, children can look into the mirror of that love and see themselves as they are today and also as they want to be in the future.

When parental love is conditional and inconstant, children become confused and are unable to move confidently toward the completeness they seek. Their self-concept suffers as they question who they are from day to day.

It was the Apostle Paul who wrote that we see imperfectly, as in a mirror that offers us dim reflections. But one day we will have full sight and knowledge and will see God face to face. Now we know in part, but then we will fully understand ourselves, even as we have been fully understood.

> One of the characteristics of the child is that he knows and understands things partially. Part of growing up into mature love is to reach a fuller, face-to-face understanding. Our pictures and our feelings about ourselves come largely from the pictures and the feelings we see reflected in our family members — what we watch in their expressions, hear from the tone in their voices, and see from their actions. These reflections tell us not only who we are, but also what we are going to become. As the reflections gradually become part of us, we take on the shape of the person we see in the family looking glass.[2]

In *Healing for Damaged Emotions*, David Seamands writes of the mirrors in amusement parks that twist our features into caricatures of ourselves. In a similar way, conditional love in the family twists a child's developing self-concept into something it was never intended to be.

> Someone has said, "Your childhood is the time of life when God desires to build the rooms of the temple in which He wants to live when you are an adult." What a beautiful thought! Parents have the great privilege, *and* heavy responsibility, of giving the basic design to the temple — the child's self-image.
>
> If he is convinced he is of low worth, a child will place little value on what he says or does. . . . If this kind of low self-esteem has been programmed into a person, it is difficult, and in some cases almost impossible, for that person to feel beloved of God, accepted by Him, and of worth to Him in His kingdom and service.[3]

Although they could not explain it clearly, children know their need of full acceptance and unconditional love. Without these, they cannot grow and develop properly.

When children cannot become what they know deep inside they should be, when they cannot be themselves, when life is a series of trick mirrors, they become angry.

As adults, we know how long it has taken some of us to feel that we can at last really be ourselves. And we know the anger we have felt at those who should have accepted and loved us without placing conditions on that love. Yet, many parents who have known the pain of not being able to develop with confidence are now withholding unconditional love from their children. In so doing, they are asking for their children's anger.

When your relationship with your children is based on conditional love, you will find it impossible to really understand your children or to give them proper guidance. You will also find parenting to be a very confusing enterprise.

But when your relationship with them is built on unconditional love, you can be confident in your parenting. With your love as a guiding light, you will be able to meet your children's needs.

PARENTS WHO PROVOKE THEIR CHILDREN

I'm sure you know the commandment God gave to Moses about honoring one's parents. Two thousand years · later, the Apostle Paul emphasized this command as he wrote to the Christians at Ephesus:

> Children, obey your parents in the Lord, for this is right. "Honor your father and mother"—which is the first commandment with a promise—"that it may go well with you and that you may enjoy long life on the earth" (Eph. 6:1-2).

But do you know what the next verse says? While we don't hear it as often, it is crucially important. I'd like you to read it in several versions of the Bible.

> Fathers, again, must not goad your children to resentment, but give them the instruction, and the correction, which belong to a Christian upbringing (NEB).

> Fathers, provoke not your children to wrath: but bring them up in the nurture and admonition of the Lord (KJV).

> You parents, too, must stop exasperating your children, but continue to bring them up with the sort of education and counsel the Lord approves (WMS).

> And you fathers, don't make your children angry, but raise them by letting the Lord train and correct them (BECK).

Fathers, don't exasperate your children by coming down hard on them. Take them by the hand and lead them in the way of the Master (TM).

It sounds as if Paul had visited in lots of homes in Ephesus, and maybe even when the parents weren't expecting him to show up. He knew what was happening in all too many families—parents were failing in patience and in training of their children. They were forgetting their long-range goal of raising mature young Christians who could in a few years be responsible men and women.

Paul was offering a balance. The responsibility for raising good children was not on the children but on the parents. Yes, the children were to obey, but the parents were responsible for their training as well as for the atmosphere of the home.

If Paul visited your home, would he say, "Don't provoke? Don't goad? Don't exasperate? Don't make them angry? Don't come down too hard on them?" A lot of provoking goes on in homes that profess to be Christian.

◆ A three-year-old girl picked a flower and brought it to her mother. Because the flower was from the neighbor's yard, the mother slapped the child and ignored the gift of love.

◆ In a snack shop, a father yelled at his young son when he saw some ice cream falling from the boy's cone onto his shirt.

◆ A mother asked her daughter, "Why can't you play the piano better, like your sister does?"

◆ A father hollered from a window to his son, "Get your friends out of our yard. They are ruining the grass!"

◆ A mother and her three-year-old son were in a mall. When the child started to wander away, the mother grabbed him and jerked him roughly, yelling, "You stay right here where I put you!"

♦ A father was kind to his son one day, but screamed at him the next, "Get your bike out of the driveway!" His mixed messages confused the boy.

If Paul were to visit your home, he wouldn't suggest ignoring bad behavior or being too lenient. But he would urge you to be constant in training your children, not only religiously but in every part of their lives.

FOCUSED TRAINING

If you have read my first book, *How to Really Love Your Child,* you already know of my emphasis on *focus* in loving and training your children. This takes the form of eye contact, physical contact, and focused attention in both listening and responding to your children. Focused love is a way of impressing deeply how much you love them.

I want us to look at each of these, especially as they apply to dealing with an angry child. It is not that hard to focus on a child who is pleasant and agreeable. But when a child is angry and rebellious, focusing with love is far more difficult. And yet, that is the challenge we all must confront again and again, as a child is growing up.

EYE CONTACT

Eye contact is one of the most powerful ways of transmitting love to a child. With eye contact, you pleasantly look into the eyes of the child while the child is looking at you. Although this sounds simple, it is actually a complex and critical behavior which is seldom done. While most parents believe they are using loving eye contact, research shows that this is not the case.

Eye contact with a child can be as simple as looking into the eyes of an adorable baby who is smiling and cooing for you. But eye contact can also be amazingly difficult. When your thirteen-year-old is angry with you and is verbalizing that anger in a loud voice at a time when you are stressed out and feel you can't handle one more thing, you probably don't even want to think about giving him loving eye contact. And yet, it is critical for you to come through at this time, for your own sake as well as for your son's. It is in situations like this that you teach him how to manage his anger in a mature fashion.

Because this type of teaching is one of the toughest parts of parenting, you need to employ self-talk during a child's angry outbursts. This technique will help you maintain self-control when you are angry. You need to remind yourself that it is normal for your child to express his anger *verbally* to you, even if it is unpleasant, for only in this way will you be able to train him to control his anger. Self-talk will keep you focused on giving your son pleasant eye contact during this difficult but important time. Regardless of his actions, it is essential to maintain eye contact with him. If he glares at you, it will be tempting to glance away. However, to avoid eye contact will further increase his anger.

With a teenager, you may run into what I call the "grunt stage." This is a period of emotional withdrawal when all you can get out of the teenager verbally is a grunt. At such noncommunicative times, the child will usually avoid eye contact. Of course, this will hamper and even hinder your ability to continue giving loving eye contact.

It is crucial that you continue to fill your child's emotional tank. You dare not dump your anger on your child. Because you want to maintain communication with him over the long haul, you need to stay in a position of training your child to manage his anger.

PHYSICAL CONTACT

When your child refuses eye contact, you do have something else at your disposal — physical contact. And yet, research shows that few children receive sufficient physical contact to keep their emotional tanks full. When everyone is feeling pleasant, giving physical contact can be rewarding to both parent and child. In times of unpleasantness, it may save the day.

With teenagers who are in the grunt stage, physical contact may be the only means of genuinely relating to them. When they are angry, they are so engrossed in their own thoughts that they are less intent on what is happening around them. At such times, gentle, light, quick touches to the back of the shoulder or arm may keep the communication open. However, if they are still angry with you, eye contact alone may have to be enough, until they calm down.

FOCUSED ATTENTION

Focused attention means spending time with a child in such a way that she feels she is the most important person in the world to you. This is most often done alone with the child. Focused attention requires sacrifice from you—the sacrifice of time. When you give this, you will also be using eye contact and physical contact.

Giving focused attention can be a real challenge, particularly if your teenager has been moody and difficult to be around. You may want to take her somewhere to improve your communication with her. You may also want to make sure her emotional tank is full. Focused attention will help you discover why she is so moody or angry.

If your child is generally unresponsive, be patient. Her silence does not necessarily mean that she is hostile or disrespectful. Teenagers often need time to pull themselves together during and after periods of anger. When you are with your child, do not pressure her to talk or respond to you. Eventually she will open up and may even allow meaningful conversation and also a resolution of her anger.

An example of focused attention during a tense situation may explain better what I mean. When our son David was thirteen, one of his best friends, Joe, invited David to spend the night. Joe's parents had recently divorced and Joe and his mother were living close enough to us to be very valued neighbors.

However, on this particular occasion, we found out that Joe's mother, Katy, was having a boyfriend over for the night. As much as we liked Katy and Joe, we just couldn't allow David to stay there overnight.

David was furious with us and refused to calm down. He assumed that we were condemning Katy, and he went to bed that night in a furor. The next day he was still angry with us, but I decided to ask if he would like to go with me to his favorite restaurant for breakfast. As we waited for our food,

David finally told me how hurt he was by not being allowed to go to Joe's house. And then he asked me what I thought about Katy's behavior.

Now I could offer an opinion that would be heard, since he had asked for it. I told him that his mother and I loved Katy and Joe as much as he did, and that we were still sad about the divorce and Joe's father moving away. I also told him that what Katy did was her own business. However, as his father, I did not feel that I would be doing my job if I permitted him to spend the night under those circumstances. Eventually David came to understand our position.

YOUR CHILD'S EMOTIONAL TANK

I have mentioned keeping your child's emotional tank full. In the context of unconditional love, the purpose of eye contact, physical contact, and focused attention is to fill your child's emotional tank. Just as a car needs gas and oil to run properly, and a furnace needs fuel, and your body needs healthful foods to function as it should, so your child needs your unconditional love, demonstrated in many ways, to become what he or she wants to be, can be, should be.

If your child has to wonder from day to day, or even hour to hour, if your love is constant or conditional, and if there is any point in trying to please you, that child will be discouraged from trying and will feel unsure of his or her own worth.

David Seamands writes of a young man named Bob who grew up in a home where "Measure Up" was the motto. He learned early in life that his measuring up was the basis for his being loved and accepted by his parents. And so he tried. Bob's parents did as so many of us do at times:

So subtly we withhold our full affection and love until we see that our children are striving at their highest level. Instead of affirming them at the level where they are, we think we are helping them to "do a little bit better." So whatever they do—eating their food or using good manners or making grades or living the Christian life on their own age level—we give our children the promise of our approval and love if only they will do a little bit better. Love becomes something just around the corner, just a hope away. The present level of achievement is subtly downgraded and belittled. We think we are saying, "We love you and want you to do better." Too often it comes across to our children as, "We will love you when you measure up," or "We will love you and be pleased with you, if only you'll do a little bit better."[4]

"The degree to which you are loved unconditionally will *determine* your level of self-esteem."[5] The same is true for your child.

Unconditional love has two fundamental qualities: (1) It is given without regard for the objective value of the person or thing which is loved; (2) It is given without any strings or conditions attached. . . . That's the kind of love which can turn your life around and raise your self-esteem level to new heights. When you find love like that, you are set free to become the person you were meant to be in all your uniqueness. And when you experience yourself in the middle of that kind of freedom, you can't help feeling good about who you find yourself to be. . . . We want to be loved *for no good reason at all.*[6]

Dr. Warren suggests that you know you have found this kind of love when you are sure that nothing you could ever do would separate you from the love the other person has for you. Such a love frees you from what Carl Rogers calls " 'conditions of worth.' You no longer have to be anything in particular in order to be loved. You can begin the journey toward self-discovery with no preset destination. In each moment you can simply be authentically yourself."[7]

To become who they are demands that your children have a strong sense of self. A strong sense of self comes from the freedom of unconditional love. And persons with a vital self-concept, nurtured in unconditional love, have the best chance of dealing well with their anger.

It is in your home that your children are learning the most important meanings of life, not only from what you say, but often from what you leave unsaid. Not only from what you do, but from what you leave undone.

It is in your home that your children are learning how much they mean to you, to God, and to themselves. Please help your children to know that they mean all the world to you, by your actions as well as your words.

Commit yourself to keeping their emotional tanks full!

UNCONDITIONAL LOVE

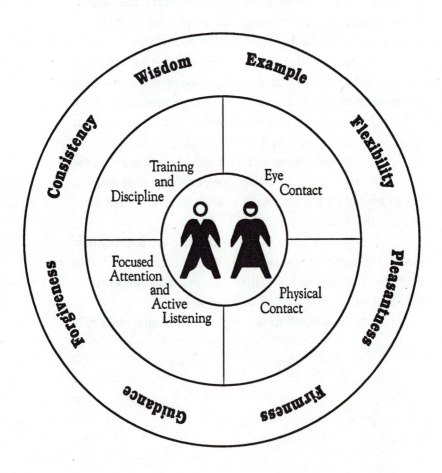

F I V E

What Is Anger?

Aggression, unconscious displays, and ventilation are three of the most common forms of handling anger for children. As we watch Jimmy, Danny, and Sue, we will see these in action.

♦ Jimmy was five years old. His teachers considered him outgoing, even-keeled, generally taking things as they come, and getting along well with other children. Yet, one day another boy accidentally pushed him down on the playground as he ran by. Jimmy reacted by attacking the boy with his fists; this left a cut over the boy's eye.

Jimmy's teachers and peers were shocked by his aggressive response. Later, his teacher learned that he was ill that day and had not been able to hold any food in his stomach. Jimmy was sorry for his behavior and apologized.

In Jimmy we see a child who normally handled his anger well. But under an adverse condition, falling ill, he allowed his anger to turn into aggression. The critical points to remember are that Jimmy was clearly conscious of his anger. He was also aware that it was wrong to hurt the other child. Even though he did not want to express his anger this way, on that day he was unable to control it.

♦ Danny, also five, was well regarded by his teachers and classmates. He had no difficulties in learning or in his relationships with other children. Yet, recently, Danny began soiling his pants with increasing frequency. Naturally, he suffered embarrassment from this humiliating pattern, but could not control it.

In Danny we see a child expressing anger unconsciously. He was unaware that he was angry and also that he was soiling himself, until it had happened. In this case, it would seem inappropriate to call his anger a feeling, since Danny didn't feel the anger. It was not evident in his behavior or his awareness, but its destructive outcome was.

♦ Six-year-old Sue is a verbal child who fluently expresses her feelings, and especially her anger. Her mother is proud of Sue's ability to verbalize. But the child has been using this ability to manipulate her mother and gain control.

As Sue expresses her anger in hostility, complaining, and arguing, her mother loses her temper and yells at Sue. Of course, this makes Sue's behavior even worse until finally her mother does one of two things. She either gives in, or she loses control and overreacts to Sue's behavior with even more intense anger which may include severe punishment.

After a short breather, the cycle begins all over again, with Sue ventilating verbally, and her mother believing that this makes Sue feel better, since her anger "should not be forced down inside of her."

Sue's mother is in a difficult position. She has fallen into the popular notion that a child should be allowed to express herself with total freedom. She fears that if Sue is forced to bury her feelings inside, her ego development will be thwarted. This "ventilation myth" is dealt with well in *The Cycle of Violence* by Suzanne R. Steinmetz.

CHILDREN ARE NATURALLY IMMATURE

Because Jimmy, Danny, and Sue are young children, they are going to handle their anger immaturely much of the time. This should be obvious, and yet, I find that many parents find it hard to accept childish forms of dealing with anger.

This lack of acceptance is a great problem for many parents. Even if they understand how to control their own anger—and few adults do—they still expect their children to handle theirs in a mature fashion. This is impossible. Most children express anger with ventilation and aggression. Unconscious expressions of anger involve suppression, and these, of course, need to be avoided.

What a dilemma! If it is unreasonable to expect our children to be mature, then it is also unreasonable to expect them to handle their anger in a mature fashion. Of course, we are not going to like their childish exhibitions of anger, but we must learn to accept them as they are, and this includes the way they express anger.

Our challenge as parents is to train our children to understand and control this anger, not all at once, but with a goal of arriving at mature expressions of anger by the time they are seventeen. This means that we will continually work at this task, dealing with our children on the age-level where they are.

Most parents have two problems with this process of training. First, they do not understand how adults should handle anger, since they generally do a poor job of this themselves. And second, they expect their children to handle anger in a mature way. When this doesn't happen, they react in a destructive manner when the child acts like a child.

There clearly is a different standard for children and adults in the handling of anger. We should have learned some things that our children don't know yet.

As we approach this difficult subject and try to find help for our homes, I want to tell you how we will proceed. In this chapter, we will be looking at what anger is, the values of anger, and some patterns of behavior common in families.

In chapters 6 and 7, we will consider the subconscious and conscious expressions of anger which are causing such havoc in increasing numbers of homes.

Because anger is a complex subject, it is not understood well, even by some of those who studied it and its results for years. What I hope to do in this book is to give you an overview that may motivate you to do further reading on your own.

In my book, *How to Really Love Your Teenager*, I included an Anger Ladder. It also appears at the end of this chapter because it shows most of the common ways of expressing anger. The number of rungs on the Ladder is unimportant. What matters is the progression upward from less acceptable forms of expressing anger to more acceptable. Healthier behaviors are printed in capital letters. At the top of the Ladder, most of the words are capped. At the bottom, none of them are. You will want to refer to the Anger Ladder as you read on.

REASONS FOR ANGER

Why do you get angry? A short answer is that you or someone you love is threatened. This threat can take many forms: physical danger, ridicule, irritation because someone has not done what he or she should have.

A threat to your selfhood or those dear to you causes anxiety. This is really a gift from God, because the combination of fear and anger at an impending threat causes you to act in readiness. Depending on the size of the threat, you may feel more fear at first, or more anger.

The threats may be to your physical well-being, your social standing, your family, your self-esteem, your economic security, your possessions, your inner peace of mind, your desires, your beliefs, or your relationships. Because these encompass most of your life, you could find yourself threatened at any point.

In a society where concerns over crime and the economy run high, and where the media reports fearful things all the time, it is natural that our self-preserving instincts also run high.

It is important that we learn to identify the sources of our anger and anxiety, so that we can better understand what is happening within us and also around us. In his book, *Coping with Your Anger: A Christian Guide*, Andrew D. Lester suggests a process to help us.

> When you are threatened, you have a natural, God-given response—you get anxious. One of the emotional parts of this anxiety is the anger that you feel. A helpful way to understand a particular experience of anger is to follow this process of evaluation. (1) I am angry, therefore I must be anxious. (2) If I am anxious, something has threatened me or something important to me. (3) What is this threat?
> ... This process can also be used to understand the anger of other people. When other people (family, friends) are angry, that means they are threatened—anxious—angry. When the threats are recognized, you can

take responsibility for dealing with your anger (and perhaps the anger of others) more creatively and ethically.[1]

THE VALUES OF ANGER

When I am angry I can write, pray, and preach well, for then my whole temperament is quickened, my understanding sharpened, and all mundane vexations and temptations gone.   Martin Luther

It is important to distinguish between the God-given emotion or response of anger and the ways we express that anger. In this book we are referring to many expressions of anger that we consider unacceptable. But for now, I want us to consider some of the values of this gift God has bestowed on us.

In an earlier chapter, I mentioned about the importance of the self-concept. We all need enough emotional and mental space to express who we are and what we can do. We all need some degree of autonomy, appropriate to our age and responsibilities. We all need to know that we are loved by someone we value. When these are threatened, we may feel angry, and this is not necessarily bad.

Children are trying to discover who they are, at the same time they are also trying to learn all about the world they are living in. It would be surprising if they and we didn't get in each other's way sometimes.

We have names for some of the most trying periods in which our children want to express their individuality. We call them "the terrible twos," "puberty," and "adolescence." What is happening in these and other difficult times of our children's lives is the push toward independence and individuation. This push is generally accompanied by some anger, as children reach for more than we think is wise at the moment. What they are saying to us is, "Pay attention to me. I don't like what you are doing. Restore my pride. You're in my way. Danger. Give me justice."[2]

We will help ourselves and our children if we can remember that this striving for a greater sense of self is fully normal and necessary. When our children know that we understand their push for more space, freedom, and authority, they will more likely work with us than against us.

Anger has so many good uses, if we know how to direct it. Think of the scientific breakthroughs that have come from someone being angry with disease and death. Or the social advances such as child labor laws, because someone was angry at children being misused.

Anger mobilizes our reserves. But what we do with those reserves is up to us. We can employ them in positive or negative ways. But first, we need to know who we are, what we want, and what is being threatened. Then we can decide how to communicate to others what we feel, as individuals or as part of a group.

This reminds me of something that happened at our Center. Marilyn, one of our wonderful social workers, passed me in the hall and I couldn't help noticing the very satisfied smile on her face. I asked her what was going on.

She told me about Dot, a young mother of three, who had been physically abused by her husband for several months. Dot had sought counsel from a Christian "celebrity" who had continually advised her to be "submissive" to her husband, no matter how he treated her. Finally, Dot's friends could no longer stand seeing her so mercilessly abused, and they brought her to our Center.

As Marilyn talked with her, she discovered that Dot

was an extremely dependent person who simply could not take steps to protect herself. However, when Dot's husband threatened to harm one of their children, she at last responded with an anger she did not feel when she was threatened and abused herself. This anger was the motivation Dot needed to take action to protect herself and her children from harm.

This story illustrates one of the prime values of anger—as a life preserver. When we are threatened, most of us determine that we are going to survive. And the heightened awareness that we gain from this anger is actually a help in planning for our survival.

One aspect of that survival is the drive to find what we are fitted for. It is often the most creative among us who have the most difficulty finding their place, their niche for expressing who they are and what they can do. When they receive little help, or downright discouragement from those close to them, they will feel angry. But their very anger may be the impetus to continue the search.

CULTURALLY LEARNED ANGER

Anger responses are often learned behavior. A distinct culture may be a tribe or community in another country, or a religious or ethnic group in our own society. Each group has its own language or meanings, and those meanings affect behavior.

Men and women are often treated as cultural groups because they tend to express emotions in different ways. "Even among young adults, thought to be more liberated from traditional sex roles, 'Women are far more likely to suppress, repress and deny anger,' says psychologist Charles Spielberger of the University of South Florida, Tampa. 'They want interpersonal harmony much more than men do, and they inhibit their anger in order to keep peace.' "³

Another cultural setting is the family, where children learn about behavior. When extended families get together, they usually behave in similar ways. This is evidenced in speech patterns and in responses to events. When you are with your extended family, you will probably see some remarkable likenesses that are also being observed and learned by your children. If those patterns include many negative expressions of anger, you can be sure your children are absorbing those too, and learning that this is how "their people" express anger.

Meg Eastman calls these "dragons that inhabit families":

> Anger patterns—each family's personal Dragons—are familiar because you probably learned them from your own parents. You saw these patterns repeated at home so many times that you automatically fell into the same behavior as you grew up. Now you may be worrying that you have become a "dysfunctional" family, despite your best intentions. Many parents find themselves handing down these Dragons to their own children and wondering, *Why is everybody so mad all the time?*⁴

If, on the other hand, your children see anger moving into positive and socially acceptable channels, they will be learning this response.

If they watch you try to understand and forgive those who have done you wrong, they will know that forgiveness is an option, not to justify the wrong but to be one element in dealing with the wrong. They will learn that anger can be controlled and expressed positively rather than negatively.

Your family is a small cultural group. Listen to its language. Watch its behavior. Discover what your children are learning about love and life and anger as they live in this culture.

What you see will at times be amusing. But it can also be downright alarming when you discover that a child really isn't all that angry, but is acting in a highly disagreeable manner because he or she has learned that this is the way to respond in a given situation.

It is possible to change such behaviors within your own household, if you are determined to do so. But don't think it will be easy. And don't assume that your extended family will praise your resolve. When you change any aspect of the family culture, you may be suspected of disturbing the cohesiveness of the family.

If you are sure that you are moving in the right direction, don't be discouraged by family members. In the long run, you will be giving something very positive to your children and, ultimately, to the extended family.

POSITIVE

1. PLEASANT • SEEKING RESOLUTION • FOCUSING ANGER ON SOURCE • HOLDING TO PRIMARY COMPLAINT • THINKING LOGICALLY

2. PLEASANT • FOCUSING ANGER ON SOURCE • HOLDING TO PRIMARY COMPLAINT • THINKING LOGICALLY

POSITIVE AND NEGATIVE

3. FOCUSING ANGER ON SOURCE • HOLDING TO PRIMARY COMPLAINT • THINKING LOGICALLY • unpleasant, loud

4. HOLDING TO PRIMARY COMPLAINT • THINKING LOGICALLY • unpleasant, loud • displacing anger to other sources

5. FOCUSING ANGER ON SOURCE • HOLDING TO PRIMARY COMPLAINT • THINKING LOGICALLY • unpleasant, loud • verbal abuse

6. THINKING LOGICALLY • unpleasant, loud • displacing anger to other sources • expressing unrelated complaints

PRIMARILY NEGATIVE

7. unpleasant, loud • displacing anger to other sources • expressing unrelated complaints • emotionally destructive behavior

8. unpleasant, loud • displacing anger to other sources • expressing unrelated complaints • verbal abuse • emotionally destructive behavior

9. unpleasant, loud • cursing • displacing anger to other sources • expressing unrelated complaints • verbal abuse • emotionally destructive behavior

10. FOCUSING ANGER ON SOURCE • unpleasant, loud • cursing • displacing anger to other sources • throwing objects • emotionally destructive behavior

11. unpleasant, loud • cursing • displacing anger to other sources • throwing objects • emotionally destructive behavior

NEGATIVE

12. FOCUSING ANGER ON SOURCE • unpleasant, loud • cursing • destroying property • verbal abuse • emotionally destructive behavior

13. unpleasant, loud • cursing • displacing anger to other sources • destroying property • verbal abuse • emotionally destructive behavior

14. unpleasant, loud • cursing • displacing anger to other sources • destroying property • verbal abuse • physical abuse • emotionally destructive behavior

15. passive-aggressive behavior

SIX

Passive-Aggressive Behavior

In this chapter and the next, we will be talking about negative expressions of anger. I want to begin with the very worst one, passive aggression.

Because everyone is passive-aggressive to some extent, none of us can claim complete freedom from this plague. However, some people are more extreme in their passive aggression, and are, therefore, easier to identify as users, and perhaps victims, of this disastrous behavior.

WHAT IS PASSIVE AGGRESSION?

Just as the name of this behavior seems contradictory, so the behavior itself is often difficult to understand and recognize. We first need to look at some definitions of the two elements, so that we will know how they combine in a most disastrous expression of anger.

In their book, *Speaking the Truth in Love: How to Be an Assertive Christian*, Ruth N. Koch and Kenneth C. Haugk help us to define passive aggression:

The word *passive* means "not resisting" or "not acting." Originally, the word *passive* was derived from a Latin word meaning "to suffer," which is an accurate description of what often results from passive behavior.

Passive behavior is behavior that moves against the self. Passive behavior says, "I'll give up anything to avoid displeasure and to gain approval." Passive performers frequently give up important parts of their own personalities to avoid disapproval or criticism, so others will like them. . . .

Aggressive behavior is behavior that moves against others. Aggressive behavior says, "I have the right to patronize you, put you down, dominate, or humiliate you in order to get what I want." The aggressive person has few internal restraints and recognizes few external limits. . . . Aggression may be expressed physically, nonverbally, verbally, and in a particular kind of aggression called passive aggression.[1]

Did you notice that passive people move against themselves? And that aggressive people move against others? Now we need to see how these two are joined.

Passive aggression is a subtle kind of aggression, an underhanded way of moving against another person or manipulating others to get one's own way. Individuals who use passive aggression are sometimes called "powerful passives" because they use undercover ways to get their own way, to get even, and to express what they are not willing to say in a straightforward manner.[2]

While passive-aggressive behavior is not that hard to define, it is difficult to identify. As parents, we need to remember that not all misbehavior is passive aggression. I want to give you three characteristics of this behavior to help you identify it in your child, or in yourself.

♦ Passive aggression is irrational and illogical. It is primarily subconscious, and the subconscious mind seldom makes sense in the outer world or depends on logical thought. The behavior is designed to be the opposite of what is expected of the person, the opposite of what he or she *ought* to do.

♦ The purpose of passive aggression is to upset the parents or other authority figures. No matter what the parents do to correct the behavior, it won't work. The more parents try to correct the situation, the more pressure they put on the child, the more determined the child is to upset them. The more the parents get upset, the more the children feel that they are succeeding. And they will try even harder to disturb the parents. The most common areas of conflict are grades and values.

We want our children to take responsibility for their own behavior, the very opposite of passive aggression. For this to happen, we need to wait until they are ready and able to do so. If we demand it before this time, they will fight us.

♦ Although the subconscious goal of passive aggression is to upset the authority figures, children ultimately hurt themselves the most by this behavior. Those who insist on getting poor grades will have to live with the results of this for the rest of their lives. Approximately one third of college freshmen flunk out every year. The vast majority of these kids are capable of making decent grades. They don't even know why they aren't making the grades of which they are capable.

Those who strike out into the more serious kinds of passive-aggressive behavior may destroy themselves with drugs, alcohol, disease and poverty, and even suicide, the ultimate passive-aggressive behavior.

ROOTS OF PASSIVE AGGRESSION

In chapter 5, we mentioned a few childish means of expressing anger. While adults should know that these are inappropriate means of dealing with anger, children do not. In their immaturity, children express their anger through ventilation and aggression. Most parents have low toleration for these means and react in ways that cause the children to handle anger in an even worse manner. When children are not trained in dealing with anger, they will not only continue to use conscious manifestations of anger but will also resort to subconscious means.

You have watched this scene: Judy is angry and sasses her mother. Her father hears her and responds in a hostile tone, "I never want to hear you talk to your mother like that again! Do you understand?"

Because she is not being taught how to deal with her anger, she learns not only that what she said is inappropriate, but also that future overt expression of anger is inadvisable, and so she begins to suppress it.

Like other young children, Judy is unable to cope with parental anger, because she has no defense against it. When her father dumps his anger on her, she is incapable of dealing with it in a mature fashion—which would keep the anger outside of her. And so, her father's anger goes right down inside of her. But it doesn't stay there.

Parental anger unloaded on the child goes down inside and comes out later in anti-authority attitudes. These attitudes are the seeds of passive aggression.

When the suppression goes on for years, and the attitudes against authority grow into adulthood, we have a full-blown passive-aggressive person who has learned well to oversuppress anger and then let it come out in ways that are nearly impossible for others to deal with.

Let's look at Marge and Jane, two young women whose parents failed to train them in appropriate expressions of anger, and who also made it clear that the two, as children, had better suppress their anger.

MARGE

Marge was a blonde, blue-eyed, attractive nineteen-year-old who was brought to me by her profoundly worried mother. As they entered my office, Marge and her mother were friendly. Both seemed eager to tell me why they were there.

Marge began by saying, "Mom and Dad are upset about my engagement to Duane. You need to know, Dr. Campbell, that Duane is black. I met him at college and I love him. He is really wonderful and I wish my parents would accept him."

Marge's mother, Ellen, replied defensively, "We don't think we are prejudiced, Dr. Campbell. We are just worried about our daughter, and also about what this marriage will mean to Duane. And we are very concerned about any children they may have."

I was deeply impressed by the sincerity of both mother and daughter, and my heart ached for them.

"Tell me about Duane," I asked.

Marge immediately said, "He's wonderful. He's smart, good-looking, sweet, kind, and he loves me."

"You're good at putting things in a nutshell," I kidded her, trying to lighten the increasingly heavy atmosphere.

"What Marge says is true, Dr. Campbell. Duane is a fine boy. But how can they face all the problems they will have in the future?"

"What does your father say about this, Marge?" I asked.

Marge's face sagged with confusion, sadness, and anger. "He is totally against the marriage and refuses to even talk about it. But I'm going to marry Duane, no matter what he says. I don't care how he feels about it." Two spots of rage reddened on Marge's young face.

A week later I saw Marge's father, Fred. He was a stern man who spoke harshly and only when he was asked a direct question. During our time together, most of what he said was negative—complaints about his wife and children and his job. It was clear that Fred was a distressed and unhappy man. He was extremely angry about Marge's relationship with Duane, and could find little good to say about either of them.

Three days later I met with Duane and saw that he was all that Marge and Ellen had said of him. He was a fine young man with a pleasant disposition. He was also bright, talented, articulate, and seemed to genuinely care for Marge.

Testing and subsequent interviews increasingly clarified the tremendous rage Marge felt toward her father. Also, we saw that she was handling her anger in passive-aggressive ways.

Over the next few weeks, Marge's academic performance deteriorated until she decided to drop out of college. Her relationship with Duane also weakened, due mainly to her changing behavior. She became increasingly passive-aggressive toward him, lying to him and then secretly dating other boys. It wasn't long before the marriage was called off.

I have known people who are in wonderful interracial and intercultural marriages. But, sadly, many romantic relationships of this type are a result of passive-aggressive behavior — an unconscious determination to upset one or more authority figures, usually the parents. When a romance is induced by such a desire, it will be destructive for the couple and also for any children they have.

Prolonged counseling was necessary before Marge could handle her anger appropriately. As she learned to express her anger in more healthy ways, she was able to gain control over passive-aggressive behavior.

JANE

Jane was one solemn-faced teenager as she entered my office. She was obviously depressed and seemed reluctant to talk, so we sat quietly for several minutes. Finally she was able to tell me how difficult it was for her to come to see me. She didn't know if she would be able to reveal her reason for being there.

After a good bit of small talk, Jane finally said that she was terribly confused about a homosexual encounter she "fell into" at college with another basketball player. She had not previously experienced anything like this, and she was deeply worried about it.

When I asked about her parents, Jane told me that her father was a successful businessman who was devoted to his wife. He was well thought of in his community and church. Jane's mother was also a fine person whom Jane loved and respected. However, both parents were very busy and spent little time with Jane. But she readily volunteered that it was "quality time." She also said that her father was easily agitated; when he became enraged with Jane, he "dumped" his anger on her.

Testing and further interviews with Jane showed that she was a deeply depressed young woman who harbored a great deal of anger. The two primary causes of her anger were her feeling of being unloved by her parents and her severe depression.

Jane had learned to process her anger in a passive-aggressive manner, and this was the source of her sexual response to her teammate. After she was treated for depression and could handle her anger in more direct and appropriate ways, she was able to better understand herself.

Jane was not a homosexual; rather, she was using passive-aggressive behavior to express her intense anger. I have seen several cases similar to this one.

ADULT PASSIVE AGGRESSION

Although Marge and Jane were beyond my target age of seventeen for the development of mature character, I was able to help them overcome their passive-aggressive behavior during an extended period of counseling.

However, when this behavior goes unchecked into adulthood, it is often also unrecognized for what it is, and can be the cause of unending frustration and pain for other people. Two areas in which it creates havoc are work and marriage.

♦ Employees with an anti-authority attitude will probably keep this hidden for the first year or two. The reason for this is that they have no cause for anger at their new employer, and so have not built up subconscious anger. Since working with and for other people has its aggravations, over time the passive aggressives will accumulate causes for anger, real or imagined, but will suppress the anger for as long as they can, usually no more than two years.

When they can suppress it no longer, it begins coming out in subconscious ways. These people are unaware that they are now determined to do the opposite of what they should be doing. The process begins with a gradual change of attitude that moves from pleasant and cooperative to difficult and annoying. Eventually they are so intolerable that they lose their jobs.

Of course, employers may also be passive aggressive, creating difficult work situations for those under them.

♦ Passive aggression can have a ruinous effect on personal relationships, and nowhere is this more evident than in marriage. At the beginning of the marriage, the person suppresses the anger, but eventually it begins to be expressed toward the spouse.

You may wonder how the passive-aggressive person is rebelling against authority within marriage. However, authority figures include not only those we are responsible to, but also those for whom we are responsible.

Marriage to a passive aggressive can resemble an ongoing nightmare with no escape, for the possibilities for upsetting the spouse are endless and reach into all areas of life. Common expressions of passive aggression in marriage are lying, physical and emotional rejection, generalized blame, mismanagement of money, and seething anger. Not exactly what people are looking for in a marriage commitment.

"NORMAL" PASSIVE AGGRESSION

There is only one time in a person's life when passive aggression could be considered "normal." That period is early adolescence, when children are thirteen to fifteen years old. The behavior stays within the range of normal as long as it does not hurt anyone and is not destructive.

It is very difficult to be a teenager today, because there are so many dangerous ways to express passive aggression. In more rural times, teens might put Farmer Brown's cow on top of the barn, or overturn a few outhouses. When I was young, we took a friend's VW beetle apart and reassembled it in his bedroom, while he was away on vacation. When my children were teens, I was grateful for pranks such as toilet-papering the yards of their friends. But today, teenagers have access to drugs, guns, alcohol, and more. The problem is compounded because so many teenagers are severely depressed.

The normal expressions of this behavior tend to start around ten or eleven years of age, when the child begins neglecting ordinary chores, dawdling, or generally upsetting the parents. When parents know that such behavior is normal, they can handle it in a healthy manner, even though it is irritating and probably will continue for a few years.

The more effectively the parents deal with the behavior, the less it will extend outside the home. If the parents are not effective, the behavior will generalize outside the home and cause embarrassing and potentially dangerous problems. Therefore, it is far better to keep most of the annoyance inside the home.

As much as you may dislike your child's messy room, you need to remember that this is far preferable to some of the other passive-aggressive expressions we have mentioned. You hope your child will curtail his angry behavior to messiness, dawdling, noise, and strange appearance at times.

It is essential to remember that when children are in the deepest stage of adolescence, they will go more for the jugular, determined to do the opposite of what the parents want. In Christian homes, this rebellion will involve the spiritual part of life, since the parents want their children to love God and faithfully attend church. In our home, we knew adolescence was upon us when on Sunday mornings we heard, "I don't want to go to church today." This, from a child who had previously been enthusiastic about church attendance.

If parents overreact or become angry, they can actually drive their children away from God permanently. We all know of Christian homes in which the grown children want little to do with the spiritual values of their parents. If you can remember that the rebellion is normal and is not against you or God or the church in a personal way, you will retain your cool on days when you could easily lose it.

Another area in which parents and young teens have conflict is about grades and academic achievement. Because the kids know that the parents are so concerned about the grades, they also know that this is a prime area in which to rebel. The chances for upsetting the parents are excellent. If parents can keep from making a huge issue over somewhat lower grades, they and their children will recover more quickly and with less unpleasantness.

You may remember that I gave you a definition of integrity in chapter 1. One element of that was to take responsibility for personal behavior. Passive aggression refuses to take responsibility and, instead, tries to place it somewhere else, on parents or the teachers. They should refuse to take it, and insist that the child retain his or her own responsibility.

A classic illustration of this happens when children are about in fifth grade. Children who have done well in school will begin to "forget" their homework. When they don't turn it in, the teacher informs the parents who then make sure that the assignment and books make it home. They think they have solved the problem, but they haven't; even though the homework is done, the kids "forget" to take it back to school. When the parents make sure it goes back, the children "forget" to turn it in, and leave it in their desks.

When my kids were in the fifth grade, I would go to the open houses and sit at some of the desks to see which children had stashed their homework there.

When my older son, David, was in eighth grade, his grades slid from A's and B's to C's. Fortunately, I knew something about normal passive-aggressive behavior at that time, and didn't react to the falling grades. He coasted through ninth grade and into tenth, when I began feeling concerned During that year, he made friends with some older boys who were about to go off to good colleges, and David became aware that his grades were important.

When he finally talked with me about the matter of grades, I could respond with my concerns. I knew he would hear me now, because he also was interested. When he asked about grade point averages to get into good colleges, I was prepared with the catalog from the school his sister was attending. He had asked her what average he would need to go there also. When he compared the requirement with his own average at the time, he was shocked and said, "Looks like I am going to have to get to work." From that day on, his grades began to improve and he was accepted at the school of his choice. If my wife and I had ranted and raved about his grades for three years, my guess is that he would have been lucky to graduate from high school.

DEALING WITH "NORMAL" PASSIVE AGGRESSION

Because dealing with "normal" teenage passive-aggressive behavior can be so provoking, it is easy for parents to move into the position of being the provoker of their children. We do this in the ways we talk to them and look at them. While these may seem insignificant in an already provoking situation, we need to remind ourselves that children cannot handle our anger. They have no mechanism to prevent it from causing harmful effects inside of them.

When parents are angry, most of them speak in a lower than normal tone. They will probably also issue commands in this tone. When they say, "I want you to empty the garbage *now*," with a lower infliction at the end, the child may automatically become angry and begin to behave in a passive-aggressive manner. I often suggest that parents take a "Yogi Bear" approach when they are angry—ending sentences with an upward inflection. This comes across as cheery and endearing rather than intimidating.

Another way that parents provoke their children is by wording something as a command rather than as a request. When we refrain from angry behavior, our children are most grateful, especially when they know that we have a right to feel angry with them.

Parents can also provoke their children by the ways they look at them, especially in a tense situation. During such times, it is critical to maintain loving eye contact and not look away from the child. But eye contact alone is not enough, for some parents keep this but look at the child in an angry or frowning manner that expresses disapproval of the child himself. The child can interpret such a look as the same as yelling or screaming. On the other hand, when a child is angry, it is important not to smile or laugh in a way that can be interpreted as ridicule.

Because looks are so important, I suggest to parents that they get in front of a mirror to cultivate the neutral look. This is particularly important if you naturally smile or frown most of the time. Without knowing it, you could seem to be ridiculing or scorning your child.

Does it sound as if I am trying to prepare you for your child's angry moments? I am. Children have the most annoying, frustrating, and totally upsetting ways of expressing their anger. When you are suddenly in the middle of such a conflict, it is difficult enough to control your own anger, much less remember to think about how you are coming across to the child.

When you are faced with an angry child, you have two obligations—to accept the child as he is, including his childish display of anger, and to express your own anger in a mature fashion. I know this is difficult, but it is so important, when you think of your goal—that your child will continually be learning to handle anger in a more mature manner. His best lessons in this ongoing education are from your example.

When a child approaches you with anger, the normal reaction is to be angry in return. But this response will not resolve the anger. You need to remember that you are the adult, and that he is the child. You should accept him as a child, but you should not copy his behavior.

If you refuse to accept the child and his childish display of anger, you are forcing the anger to go somewhere else, and the only place it can go is inside. This is setting the child up for passive-aggressive behavior now and in the future.

ASCENDING THE ANGER LADDER

I'm sure you saw the Anger Ladder in chapter 5. As you work with your children in the coming years, you will always be seeking to help them climb from one rung to the next, away from the negative expressions of anger to the more positive. This is a long process that involves both training and example.

You'll notice that passive aggression is at the bottom of the Ladder. If you have thirty rungs or sixty, passive-aggressive expressions of anger will always be at the bottom. Because passive aggression is common to teenagers, every parent has to deal with this form of anger. The key thing is that you don't let your child stay there.

You need to remind yourself that your child can climb only one rung at a time. This fact is frustrating to parents who want the process to be over soon. What is even more frustrating is that parents have to wait until a child is ready to take the next step. This calls for patience and wisdom. But I can tell you that the results are well worth the wait. Pat and I have seen our three children move to mature expressions of anger, as we let them grow at their own pace.

When you watch your child express anger, you'll want to identify where he or she is on the Ladder. Then you will know the next step. My most unpleasant experience of a child speaking to me in a very inappropriate manner was with David when he was about thirteen. Thank goodness the phase didn't last long. His unpleasant verbalization of anger occurred only when a particular event upset him. When he was verbalizing his anger at me in ways that I didn't want to hear, I had to do some self-talk to determine where he was on the Anger Ladder. I would say to myself, "Attaboy, David, Attaboy. Let that anger out, because when it is all out, I've got you." Of course, I didn't say any of this to David.

The reason I wanted the anger to come out was that as long as the anger was inside of him, it controlled the house. But once the anger was outside, then he felt silly, and I could regain control. He had gotten all the anger out verbally and was asking himself, "Now what do I do?" It was then that I was in a great position to train David.

Another reason I was glad to see it come out was that the more anger that came out of his mouth, the less there would be to come out in lying, stealing, sex, drugs, and all the other passive-aggressive behaviors going on today.

Fellow parent, I know that this is not easy to grasp, and you may have serious questions at this point. Allowing a child to express his or her anger is not being permissive. We must remember that children of any age will naturally express anger in immature ways. We cannot train them to express their anger in mature ways simply by getting upset and forcing them to stop expressing their anger. If we do this, their anger will be oversuppressed, and passive-aggressive behavior will then result.

If we want to train our children to express anger in a mature fashion, we must allow them to express it verbally, even though that may be unpleasant. Why? The best way to express anger is *verbally and pleasantly*, but children can't learn to do this if they are not allowed to verbalize it at all. Therefore, wise parents will want their children to express anger verbally, first, to prevent them from oversuppressing it, and second, to lead the children up the rungs of the Anger Ladder.

All anger must come out either verbally or behaviorally. If we don't allow it to come out verbally, our children must oversuppress the anger, and passive-aggressive behavior will be the result.

When your child brings anger to you in a verbally unpleasant way, it does not necessarily mean that the child is being disrespectful. To determine whether this is so, ask yourself, "How is this child's attitude toward my authority most of the time?" Most children are respectful over 90 percent of the time.

If this is true of your child, and now he or she is bringing verbal anger to you about a particular situation, this is just what you want to happen. You know what to do—and you are not alone. You have "Yogi Bear," eye contact, the neutral look, and self-talk with you. When your child has gotten the angry feelings out, you are then in an excellent position to train your child. In chapter 9, we will talk more about specific ways to train your child. For now, just a reminder that your own behavior during a child's anger is most critical.

It may seem unfair that when a child comes to you in anger, you are supposed to feel thankful that the child is expressing the anger verbally and then control yourself. I know it is not easy, but as you behave this way, you force yourself to mature. You also are saving yourself and your children from some of life's worst problems later on.

You may be asking, "What about the child who verbalizes anger most of the time, even when he is not upset about a particular event?" Some children use ventilation of anger to manipulate their parents and get their own way. This is quite different from anger at a specific situation. Such ventilation, with a motivation to upset and hurt others, is inappropriate and must be corrected. But in doing so, the same parental parameters apply: We must be pleasant but firm.

What I encountered with David was not ventilation but normal teenage anger. However, I would not want to leave the impression that I felt no tension or anger myself. And I had to let that die down before I could work with David. There is no one right way to work with a child, and you may find better methods than I did. The main thing is to keep your objective in mind.

When your child brings his anger to you, he is also bringing himself to be trained. It is crucial not to begin training your child until both of you have calmed down and reestablished a good feeling between you. It is also crucial that you don't wait too long, or you will lose the effect of building on what happened. As soon as things are stable between you, sit down together and do three things.

♦ You want to let him know that you are not going to condemn him. Especially if a child is very responsive to authority, a 25 percenter (see chap. 11), he may feel guilty about what he has done. Unless I let him know that I am not going to condemn him, he may never do it again. But if he never does it again, I won't have the opportunity to help him climb the Anger Ladder. Part of training is letting him know that I accept him as a person and always want to know how he is feeling, whether happy or sad or angry. And so I say to David, "When you are angry, I want to know that you are."

♦ Next, you want to commend your child for the things he did right. And so with David, I said, "You did let me know that you were angry, and that is good. You didn't let your anger out on your little brother or the dog. You didn't throw anything or hit the wall. You simply told me that you were angry."

Do you see where I am going with this? Whatever he did that was right I mentioned. Any time a child brings verbal anger to you, he has done some right things and avoided some wrong ones.

♦ Next, you want to help your child take a step up on the Anger Ladder. This involves giving a request rather than a prohibition. Instead of saying, "Don't ever call me that name again!" you say, "From now on, Son, please don't call me that name. All right?" Now this doesn't guarantee that he will never again say what you have asked him not to. But it does ensure that when he is sufficiently mature, he will take that step. It may be the next day or several weeks or months down the road. This kind of training is a long and difficult process.

After you have gone through the process enough times, your child will begin to do some thinking without your reminder. The combination of your training plus your good example of handling anger in a mature way will help your child to do his or her own self-training after a while.

The most crucial element here, as in all areas of dealing with your children, is to give them unconditional love. When they know that they are loved in this way, when they truly feel loved all the time, they will be far more responsive to your training. And you will be much more likely to achieve your goal of maturity by age seventeen.

SEVEN

More Immature Expressions of Anger

Although passive aggression is the worst expression of anger, there are other forms which can cause tragic harm to both individuals and families.

As a person matures, the way he handles his anger should also mature. But the fact is that we see many adults who are dealing very badly with their anger, and then teaching these behaviors to their children, consciously or by example. In this chapter we will be looking at some destructive forms of anger.

AGGRESSION

The purpose of aggression is to cause harm to a person or object or group. It can be expressed verbally or physically. For example, a child may attack with weapons, words, hands, or feet. The use of aggression is almost always inappropriate and usually results in irreparable harm in relationships. Any apparent gain will eventually be overshadowed by destructive consequences.

These consequences are especially serious between parents and children. Aggressive behavior on the part of parents toward their children will most certainly result in rebellion against authority. Also, the parents are failing as role models when they teach their children to use aggression.

If you look back to the Anger Ladder, you will see that aggressive actions are toward the bottom of the scale, and are usually combined with other destructive behaviors.

Living as we do in an extremely aggressive society, we know that violence begets violence. Watching others commit aggressive acts, in person or on the screen, increases one's chances of behaving aggressively.

I was particularly impressed with the findings of Dr. Leonard D. Eron, psychology professor at Yale University, in his study of causes of aggression in children. As he observed them over two decades, he found two things to be true: Those children who watched more television used more aggression; and the more television they watched, the more likely they were to become aggressive adults who would commit crimes.

As the subjects of his study were approaching thirty years of age, Dr. Eron revisited them and discovered that his earlier findings were indeed true.[1]

Of course, the problem is complex and cannot be placed solely on the amount of television a child watches. I believe the most critical component in determining how a person will eventually express anger is the degree of anti-authority bias in his or her makeup. That is, the amount of passive aggression that underlies expressions of anger.

In chapter 6, we pointed out the difference between aggression and assertiveness. This needs to be emphasized again, because assertive behavior is usually healthy and appropriate. Assertiveness is the direct expression of feelings, including anger, but without the intent to hurt another.

When it is expressed constructively, assertiveness can go a long way toward achieving a person's goals.

Aggression, however, is intended to cause harm, through violence to a person, to property, or both. In *Taming the Dragon in Your Child*, Meg Eastman includes a chapter titled, "The Aggressive, Out-of-Control Child," in which she offers helpful suggestions. After detailing specific behaviors such as fighting, blaming, and power struggles, she says:

> The problems of aggressive, out-of-control children may have stemmed originally from stress, impulsiveness, over-activity, abuse, or lack of training in self-control. It is often easy to excuse and overlook aggression in young children. However, by school age, their anger patterns often reach disturbing levels.
>
> These children may relish the power and control their aggressive outbursts achieve. They may show no remorse or conscience and may not care about how their behavior affects others. In fact, they often look for another person to blame for the problem. Refusal to accept responsibility is characteristic. . . .

Typical situations that trigger the anger of an aggressive child include:

♦ Anything that threatens to lower his sense of status and control.

♦ Being exposed as a failure in class or on a sports team, within his family or peer group.

♦ Challenges to his power base — not being able to have his way, having to follow a class rule, or to complete an assignment that "bores" him.[2]

Meg Eastman believes that the aggressive child needs "limits, limits, and more limits!" She offers valuable guidelines for discipline. If you have this problem in your home, I hope you will read her book.

VENTILATION

Ventilation is a verbal expression of anger. It differs from verbal aggression in that its intent is not to bring harm to another person, but simply to get rid of one's anger. This type of behavior may range from loud, angry screaming to muttered expletives, from complaining and arguing to hysterical tirades.

Regardless of how it comes out, ventilation of anger is unpleasant to be around and is definitely a behavior we want our children to outgrow by the time they are seventeen.

However, as disagreeable and immature as ventilation is, it serves a purpose in childhood, because it presents us with something we need in order to train our children about anger. As long as they are expressing anger *verbally*, they probably are not expressing it *behaviorally*, as in aggression or passive aggression.

We parents need to remember that anger comes out in only two ways—verbally or behaviorally—and we have a good deal of control over which of these two ways our children use. Most children employ verbal expressions of anger. The more parents prevent this expression, by telling children, "Shut up!" or "Never talk that way again!" the more the anger will come out behaviorally.

If we parents truly understand that we have a choice in determining how our children express anger, we will be glad, relatively speaking, to have them use verbalizations rather than physical aggression or passive aggression.

NAGGING AND WITHHOLDING

Nagging is an immature expression of anger that is closely related to ventilation. Yet, it differs from ventilation in that it has a purpose other than merely getting rid of anger. We nag when we feel ineffective or powerless in controlling or influencing another person or a situation. It is most common in close relationships, like the family.

Nagging is an underhanded way of saying, "I just want to help you." We parents must remember that nagging is a subtle way of dumping our anger on a child. It is highly destructive and is a sure way to push the child toward anti-authority attitudes.

Withholding can be a legitimate means of disciplining a child, or it can be an expression of anger. As a form of discipline, a parent may temporarily withhold something the child wants. As long as it is not done to hurt the child or accompanied by continued parental anger, this can be an appropriate means of punishment.

However, an angry parent may withhold affection and nurture. This is particularly dangerous, because the child then learns how to use this treacherous behavior and will probably employ it passive-aggressively by withholding affection, obedience, achievement, cooperation, pleasantness, and more.

SILENCE AND WITHDRAWAL

Silence and withdrawal are inappropriate ways to handle anger. They can be especially harmful in a marital relationship, when they are used to conceal anger.

We may use silence and withdrawal to avoid admitting we are angry and also to avoid confronting the situation and the other person in a healthy way. These devices are closely related to withholding; however, in silence and withdrawal we shut ourselves off from the relationship. Most people who engage in these adverse behaviors are unaware of just what is happening.

Silence and withdrawal are very harmful to a child because they are the opposite of unconditional love. To withdraw from the parent/child relationship is the same as telling the child, "Sometimes I love you, sometimes I don't." This classic example of conditional love is one of the greatest sources of anger and rage from child to parent. Dear parents, we must not fall into this immature and harmful behavior, with our children or in our marriages. The results are disastrous!

Writing from painful personal experience, Andrew D. Lester tells how he and his wife learned to deal with their anger constructively, instead of retreating into silence.

> Instead of being so afraid of our anger, we began to take the risk of sharing it with each other as we did our other thoughts and feelings. We started taking responsibility for using anger constructively instead of allowing it to rob us of our happiness. We know now that anger has the potential for increasing intimacy in close relationships.[3]

DISPLACED ANGER

Displaced anger uses innocent people as targets. This most often occurs when we are angry at someone we cannot confront with our rage—an employer, professor, or superior. Displaced anger is quite easily vented on children.

When a child's immaturities annoy the parent, instead of handling this anger in loving and instructive ways, the parent may dump hostility from other sources on the child.

It is crucial to remember that children cannot tolerate parental anger, because they have no defenses against it. Dumping any anger on them is injurious, but dumping excess rage from other sources can be truly destructive. When we parents learn to control ourselves, positive control of our children's development will naturally follow.

OVERSUPPRESSED ANGER VERSUS VENTILATION

There is much confusion today about the suppression of anger. One school of thought advocates that feelings should never be suppressed or bottled up. Followers of this school believe that feelings, and especially anger, should be ventilated. In the 1960s and 1970s we heard a good deal about ventilation, and Theodore Rubin's *The Anger Book* is still a popular advocate of this position.

There *is* truth in the belief that oversuppressing anger in the subconscious mind may result in various problems, such as psychiatric illness and passive-aggressive behavior. Suppression of anger is also related to certain types of physical illness. In their research on suppression, Howard Friedman and Stephanie Booth-Kersley observed that the following emotions have been implicated in physical illness: anger, depression, hostility, anxiety, and introversion. In their statistical analysis of the results of 101 studies, they determined these five diseases to have emotional components: heart disease, ulcers, headaches, arthritis, and asthma.[4]

However, to simply ventilate anger does not alleviate or prevent these problems. In fact, ventilation as a means of getting rid of anger cannot only cause the problems I have just mentioned, but may also increase rageful feelings. In all too many cases, it is like throwing gasoline on a fire.

Because the case for ventilation has been so publicized in psychological circles, I want to underscore it further. Advocates of this position believe that "getting it out of your system" is always beneficial. However, this view "tends to overlook the social context and the consequences of anger. If your expressed rage causes another person to shoot you, it won't matter that you die with very healthy arteries."[5]

Carol Tavris offers us three myths of expressed anger in *Anger: the Misunderstood Emotion.*

Myth #1: "Aggression is the instinctive catharsis for anger."

Myth #2: "Talking out anger gets rid of it—or at least makes you feel less angry."

Myth #3: "Tantrums and other childhood rages are healthy expressions of anger that forestall neurosis."[6]

I can include only a fragment of her answer to each of these and I urge you to read her excellent book. Her response to these three myths:

#1: "When you permit children to play aggressively, they don't become less aggressive, as the catharsis theory would predict; they become more aggressive. . . . Verbal aggression usually fails because it riles up the other person and makes him or her inclined to strike back."[7]

#2: "Talking out an emotion doesn't reduce it, *it rehearses it.* . . . Talking can freeze a hostile disposition. This is true for children, teenagers, and adults alike. . . . Children who were encouraged to express their anger toward the child who had frustrated them later liked that child less than the children who were *not permitted* to express their anger!"[8]

#3: " 'Expressing anger' is not the same as 'acting aggressively,' but many parents, eager not to block the former, encourage the latter. When you allow a child to scream, kick, hit, or smash objects, however, you are not reducing the child's anger. You are increasing his aggressiveness."[9]

SELF-ABUSE

Although the growing tendency in our society is to blame others for one's problems, there are still many people who put themselves down when things go wrong.

Some send negative messages to themselves. The more they do this, the more they take life too seriously and personally. A few people are real champions at this.

Most of those who turn their anger inside do not feel the anger. Rather, they feel "hurt." They find ways to blame themselves for any problem and are quite prone to guilt. This habit of putting themselves down may cause despair, depression, and feelings of helplessness and hopelessness. Because depression is a major source of anger, a destructive cycle can result from this type of self-abuse.

People who tend to handle anger by directing it to the self usually fall into this trap when they have lost control over something such as a close relationship, their business, or money matters. They believe the situation is unmanageable.

The answer as to why some people handle anger in this way is complex. Part of it is genetic—certain personality types are more prone to direct their anger inside. Also, it is common to inadvertently train our children to handle anger this way. If we criticize and blame them, they may respond by criticizing and blaming themselves and may also develop the habit of directing the anger inward. This is especially true of 25 percenters. The 75 percenters, in contrast, will respond by "identifying with the aggressor": they will mimic the parents by criticizing and blaming someone else. These children may develop habits of refusing to take responsibility for their own behavior and of blaming others. Both means of handling anger are destructive.

Self-abuse is aggravated by passive-aggressive attitudes. For example, as the depression deepens and causes anger, a desire for revenge can form and grow. Finally, even suicidal thoughts and attempts may result. Suicide is the ultimate passive-aggressive act: "You'll be sorry when I'm gone!"

It is important to remember that all of these immature expressions of anger can be employed by both children and adults. This means that we parents will want to identify those we are using and then correct them, so that we can train our children to handle their anger correctly.

There are, of course, other inappropriate and harmful ways to express anger. But most of them are related to those we have mentioned. When you learn how to deal with the most basic ones, you can apply your knowledge to other behaviors.

EIGHT

Parents, Cure Yourselves!

Whether we like it or not, we parents have the greatest influence on our children — for good or bad. And the factor which has the most influence on them is the way we manage our anger. It is a double whammy. Our management of anger becomes an example for them to follow, and it also affects them in several critical ways.

Inappropriate control of our anger hurts our children's self-esteem, sense of identity, ability to relate to others, perceptions of the world, stress management, and overall ability to function in society. Also, our mismanagement of anger causes our children to develop passive-aggressive, anti-authority, self-defeating attitudes, which, if not corrected by their late teen years, will become deep-seated factors in their basic character.

If we handle our own anger maturely, we give our children one of the greatest and most caring gifts there is. This gift is a potent life force that will assure that they grow to their own maturity without the afflictions so many adults struggle with today.

One of the most wonderful experiences in life is to see our children develop into warm, caring, conscientious, energetic, motivated, respected, and well-liked adults.

The reason parental management of anger is so important is that children are so sensitive toward their parents' anger. It is impossible for them to pass it off or to take it casually. Even one incident of mismanaged anger will cause extreme pain, just as mature handling of anger can intensify the love between parents and children.

Every day we parents face situations in which we have a choice as to how we will handle our own anger. If we behave in a mature way, we will strengthen the bonds between us and our children. We may not immediately sense the increased respect and appreciation in the hearts of our children, but over the years we will find parenting to be ever more satisfying and fulfilling. If, however, we dump anger on our children, we will weaken the bonds of affection.

Before you can effectively train your children in their management of anger, you first need to look at yourself. That is what this chapter is about. In fact, I recommend that you read this chapter and the next one before you go to sleep at night. After a couple of readings, you will be able to review them in a few minutes. As you read each evening, you can then pledge yourself to handle your anger well for the next twenty-four hours. Every day you do this is like putting money in the bank to insure a secure future for you and your children. But, every day you handle anger poorly is like losing money and jeopardizing the future for your family.

TWENTY QUESTIONS

Do you remember the old television game show "Twenty Questions"? I have twenty questions for you to answer. They aren't as entertaining as those on the TV show, and they will take time to answer thoughtfully, but I can promise you that the rewards will be much greater than from any game.

As you read and answer the questions, take a moment to reflect on those areas where you may not be doing as well as you would like. For instance, you may take responsibility for your behavior most of the time, but in certain circumstances you fall down. If that is so, you need to ask yourself why that happens.

1. Do you take responsibility for your behavior?
2. Do you keep your promises?
3. Do you feel generally positive about your character and level of maturity? Or, do you feel negative?
4. Are you usually optimistic? Or pessimistic?
5. Are you still struggling with attitudes and events from your childhood and teenage years?
6. Do you often feel anger you cannot resolve?
7. Do you like who you have become? Do you have a plan for continued growth?
8. Does the idea of getting to know yourself better sound like a good adventure or a dangerous threat?
9. Do you show respect and fairness to each member of your family?
10. Do you show respect and fairness to those whom you manage at work? At church or in the community?
11. Do you often complain about those who are over you at work? In the church or community?
12. Do you give an honest day's work for your pay?
13. Do you frequently complain about your spouse?
14. Do you recognize and cultivate the presence of God in your marriage and family life? In your personal life?

15. Do you have an ongoing plan for training your children in all areas of their lives, including the spiritual? Does this plan involve people in your extended family, church, and community?
16. Do you want your children to develop a character like yours?
17. When you face problems, do you generally ignore them or do you think and pray about how you can confront and resolve them?
18. Are you open to new ideas and developments? Or, do you find change threatening?
19. Are there people from whom you should ask forgiveness?
20. Are there matters for which you should make restitution?

If you have difficulty with some of these questions, that is all right, as long as you admit it and are willing to work to become a more mature person. If problem areas came to mind, you may want to write them down and spend some time considering what you need to do to grow or change. Pray about these areas, perhaps with your spouse or a friend, and trust that God will be with you in your desire to become more like what He intends.

TAKING RESPONSIBILITY
FOR YOUR OWN ANGER

In chapters 6 and 7, we talked about how not to manage anger. Now we need to talk about how we should be managing it.

The first step is a willingness to be responsible for our anger. This is difficult, because it is so easy to blame someone or something else for "making me mad" and to hold them responsible for what the anger "made" us do. Unfortunately, most people use their anger as an excuse for whatever they want to justify—their actions or attitudes. In fact, most people consciously or unconsciously seek out reasons to get angry, so that they may then justify their own wrongdoing!

Over the years, I have known of employees who have been fairly treated by their employers, and yet have caused devastating harm to them. In each case, the employees used trivial and unrelated occurrences to justify their anger, and then used that anger to justify their irresponsible behavior.

To take responsibility for anger, we must first identify it. Many people do not even realize when they are angry. One reason for this is that they may feel jealous, frustrated, or hurt, and are not aware that the basis of those feelings is anger.

But even if these adults are not conscious of their anger, we can be sure that their children are. When parents refuse to deal with the anger, their children feel less respect for them. But when the parents identify their anger, then they are able to name it, to admit, "I am angry." Only then can they assume responsibility for it.

No one can take responsibility for your anger but *you.* When you blame someone else for it, you give that person the power to upset you. Your anger is *your* responsibility. And how you handle and express that anger is also *your* responsibility.

Blaming your child for your anger is inexcusable. It is also dangerous, because you will naturally blame the child for anger caused by totally unrelated situations. For example, you may have had an angry disagreement at work which you did not resolve but simply "forgot." You get home and your child's behavior upsets you. If you blame your child for your anger, you will probably also blame him for your earlier encounter at work. This sets you up to dump accumulated anger on your child. Without doubt, the results will be tragic, especially if you continue to use your child as a dumping ground for your accumulated anger.

DEALING WITH YOUR ANGER

Since we all get angry every day, we need some means of coping with it, so that it doesn't get the best of us.

♦ Because you don't feel proud of yourself when your anger gets out of control, it is easy to want to "forget" what happened. However, it is important to identify and also to remember your anger. You want to remember how you behaved, or you are later likely to displace your anger on someone else, or oversuppress it and then become passive-aggressive.

I recommend keeping a notebook of your progress in coping with anger. For instance, if your boss or someone else treats you unfairly and you feel deeply hurt (angry), you may not be in a position to confront or deal with the hurt. But you can log the incident in your notebook and later record how you resolved the problem.

Just how do you resolve it? Remember, the best way to handle anger is verbally, pleasantly, and directly with the person you are angry at. If possible, you want reconciliation and greater understanding between you.

If your problem is with a manager at work, and if it is appropriate to confront this person, you will want to do so in a calm and controlled manner. You will express your concern and then listen to the response. If the response is mature and you can together negotiate a solution, that's great.

However, if you confront and the response is immature, and no solution is forthcoming, don't despair. And don't ventilate. Seek out a friend or your spouse or a counselor with whom you can *share* your feelings, not ventilate. Remember, ventilation increases the anger. Yet, if you keep it all inside, you will oversuppress it. Sharing your feelings with a trusted person will help.

Some people find relief in writing their feelings. I have counseled some folks to write a letter to the person with whom they are angry. But don't be in a hurry to mail the letter. It is usually better to throw it out after you feel more calm.

♦ I would now like to suggest some ways of reducing your proneness to anger. The better your condition physically, spiritually, emotionally, the more effective you will be in handling anger.

It is obvious that the body needs a healthy and balanced diet. We hear so much about this that I hardly need to say more. However, one little-known study has shown that too little fat in the diet can cause anxiety and irritability in some people. Your body needs an adequate amount of fat to remain healthy. I see increasing evidence of the wrong kind of dieting in my practice with behaviorally disturbed people. It is generally recommended that the fat in our diets should be 30 percent of our total caloric intake.

This, of course, reminds us of the growing problem on the other end of the spectrum, in that many Americans are becoming increasingly overweight and out of shape.

Spiritual health is just as crucial for balance as good diet and physical fitness. I have discovered that far too often in my own experience. We all need to make regular times for prayer, confession, reading the Scriptures, fellowship with other Christians, and church attendance.

♦ A common cause of anger is depression. This is a vicious cycle, because depressed people have increased problems in controlling their anger. If you think depression may play a part in your feelings and behavior, you need to seek help.

Children are acutely sensitive to depression in a parent. Also, parental depression can cause enumerable problems in the parent-child relationship, as well as in the child's development. Depressed behavior by the parent may cause guilt in the child, especially in a 25 percenter. This makes it hard for a parent to set and enforce limits.

WHEN YOU DO GET ANGRY, THEN WHAT?

When you are with your child and something happens that results in your feeling angry, how should you handle it? If you can stay within these three words—FIRM BUT PLEASANT—you are doing fine.

Remember, children are very aware of any anger or irritations you are feeling, and they are fearful that you will dump on them. When you are angry, they know it, and they feel profoundly relieved and grateful when you remain pleasant.

But, you are human, and sometimes you will lose it and risk dumping on your child. What do you do then? What I do in such times is to use self-talk. I tell myself something like, "You're losing it, Campbell. Don't make a fool of yourself and say something you will have to apologize for later.

Cool it!" That usually works. I might also say to myself, "If you don't want your children to be passive-aggressive and develop into irresponsible adults, you had better behave yourself."

If self-talk doesn't calm me down, I try to get away immediately. One ploy which has never failed me is to say, "I've got to go to the bathroom. I'll be back." And I go right to the bathroom. My children never followed me in, although some friends have told me that their young children have.

When I am alone, I think about the situation—how and why I got so angry and how I can handle it to make it a positive learning experience for everyone, including me. It helps to think of a funny incident from the past that involves the child I am currently dealing with. Not only does this calm me down, but it brings up pleasant feelings toward the child. What I am really doing is giving myself a time-out, just as we do for young children. Later, I confer with my wife to get her perspective. This usually helps me to handle the next encounter better.

When you get angry at a child, and in the tension of the situation have said or done something you regret, you have a great opportunity to make good come out of bad. One wonderful thing you can do is to ask your child's forgiveness. This teaches your child to forgive—not only you but himself as well. Your example of receiving forgiveness shows your child how to do this. In our world of so many miserable people who cannot forgive others or themselves, what a valuable lesson you are giving your child!

There are few genuine pearls of wisdom, but here is one I learned many years ago from a wise professor: "True intimacy comes from resolved conflict." This is just as true in the parent/child relationship as it is in marriage. This priceless pearl has removed my fear of conflict and of anger in my family relationships. It could "almost" make me look forward to conflict, because true intimacy follows in its wake.

When a conflict arises in our home, I see it as an opportunity to draw us closer together. But in order to resolve a conflict, I must first be able to handle my anger. If I can express it verbally and pleasantly and resolve the conflict, I will see our relationships grow and flourish.

WHEN MOTHER IS THE TARGET OF A CHILD'S ANGER

Let's assume that you have done your best to provide a loving and relaxed home atmosphere for your growing children. You and your spouse are growing in your marriage relationship and moving toward greater levels of acceptance and forgiveness and mutual support.

Even in such a home, perhaps especially in such a home, one childhood behavior can cause great distress to mothers. Often a child will express more anger at one parent than the other, and the mother is usually the target. I have talked with many wonderful mothers who interpret this as negative, and consider themselves "bad" mothers. This can result in guilt and depression. And yet, in most homes the child's behavior is not only normal, but indicates that the mother is doing her job beautifully.

In the majority of cases, the mother is the only person in the world with whom the child feels so loved and secure that he feels safe in expressing negative feelings. He knows that no matter how he behaves or what he says, Mother will always love him and never reject him. That is a wonderful assurance that mothers need to understand. Of course, this doesn't mean that the mother should permit inappropriate expressions of anger and do nothing about them.

What it does mean is that the child's confidence in the mother's love sets the stage for training. As long as the child is bringing his anger to his mother *verbally*, she and the father are in the position for training this child to handle his anger correctly.

If the child were unable to express anger verbally to the parents, they would have no means to train him. You see, the child's anger must come out somewhere. We want it to come out verbally, and it usually does so to the mother. That it happens this way does not mean that she is doing anything wrong or that the father is a better parent.

In single-parent homes, especially when the mother is the custodial parent, even more of the anger will be directed at her. Not only is anger drawn to her for the same reasons given above, but also because a single mother is around the child more. This is an example of passive-aggressive behavior raising its ugly head, making an already difficult situation even worse. The child is angry at the divorce but is taking it out on the mother.

When a child, and especially a teenager, is around one parent more than the other, the child will express more anger at that parent. Because the noncustodial parent spends less time with the child and is therefore less involved with discipline and other conflict situations, he will receive much less anger. This will make it appear as if the child is better behaved with this parent, usually the father. It then can be misinterpreted that the noncustodial parent is a "better parent." This makes the mother's job even more difficult. I have often seen this phenomenon used against the custodial parent in court.

It is critical for a mother who has custody to understand what we have just discussed, to maintain her courage
and hope, and to prevent feelings of guilt and discouragement. She should remember that while she may seem to have
an unfair disadvantage—and in some ways she does—if she
will handle her own anger and her child's anger well, in the
long run she will win the deepest respect and love from the
child. That's a promise!

NINE

Training Your Child

As our society continues to lose its spiritual and moral direction, conscientious parents cannot leave the ethical education of their children to other people. We cannot count on a consensus of values that we once took for granted, from schools, churches, and other institutions. In saying this, I am not suggesting that there are no positive influences. But I am saying that there is alarming confusion today about basic right and wrong, in all segments of our society. As columnist Ellen Goldman writes, "At some point between Lamaze and the PTA, it becomes clear that one of your main jobs as a parent is to counter the culture."[1] This means that we parents need to assume responsibility for the total education of our children.

One of our most important responsibilities as parents is to teach our children to *think rationally*. They need to be able to evaluate and judge for themselves by the time they reach adolescence, since they then have such strong outside influences pulling them in directions that often are not good for them.

I have seen far too many dear parents in agony when they discovered the moral state of their children. Their teens had been subtly taught by those around them to rationalize their behavior. They were able to justify destructive acts such as illegal drug use, drinking, and premarital sex.

At the base of these rationalizations were two factors — passive-aggressive anger and a lack of parental training. Some parents think their children are automatically going to be able to think clearly, just because they are gathering information in school. But being filled with facts does not make one wise.

Parents need to intentionally teach their children how to think in correct and rational ways, at the same time they are teaching them how to handle their anger. This is not easy, because there are increasing numbers of sociopaths in our society and our children may meet these people anywhere — even in church.

READING TOGETHER

One of the most pleasant and valuable ways of helping your children to learn to think clearly is to read together, starting in infancy.

You will want to select stories and songs and poems that are appropriate and enjoyable for the age-level of your children, for this should be a warm, bonding time together with your children. Many stories have strong ethical and moral lessons, such as *Pinocchio* and *Peter Rabbit*. And, of course, you will want to have a Bible story book that your children can understand.

In *Honey for a Child's Heart*, Gladys Hunt provides a guide to children's classics. To help parents distinguish between a good book and one lacking significant value, she writes, "A good book has a profound kind of morality — not a cheap, sentimental sort which thrives on shallow plots and superficial heroes, but the sort of force which inspires the reader's inner life and draws out all that is noble."[2]

I also recommend *Books That Build Character* by William Kilpatrick and Gregory and Suzanne M. Wolfe, because the authors provide an extensive list of books and stories, as well as a rationale for using literature in teaching moral values.[3]

A more recent addition is William Bennett's *The Book of Virtues*, a collection of stories and other selections chosen for enjoyable family reading and also as a basis for discussions together about values and morality.[4]

As you read with your child, be alert to her reactions. When the child responds to a story, ask what she is thinking; this will enable you to enter the discussion on her interest level. For example, if you are reading about a little girl who got lost, and your child expresses concern for the girl, you have a wonderful opportunity to say how good it is that she is caring and kind.

This means of teaching children is especially critical in helping them *handle blame and criticism*—both toward themselves and toward others. Inappropriate blaming is typical in children: "It's not fair. He started it!" Here is where anger can confuse a child's thinking. It is common for children and immature adults to believe that blaming another person is justified, simply because they feel angry. This is a critical opportunity for parents to help their children think rationally.

When a child is calm and able to understand, a parent can review the situation, carefully explaining all sides of the issue. They are then teaching the child to understand the other person's point of view. Storytime may be a good setting in which to do this. Parents need to remember that it takes years to be able to handle blame and criticism well. As a child matures in this area, he will assume more responsibility for his own behavior.

Another important kind of learning through reading is to widen a child's world so that he understands life from other points of view. This means that you have the rare opportunity to teach your child empathy and sympathy—two qualities that are rare today.

Empathy is seeing and entering into a situation from another's point of view. *Sympathy* is understanding the feelings of another. It does not imply agreement with the other person, nor does it mean that we necessarily feel as they do. In learning to understand another person's situation and feelings, a child can become more fair-minded, encouraging, comforting, and compassionate.

I was proud of my six-year-old granddaughter, Cami. In her school class was an unfortunate child who was disliked and rejected by most of the children. Cami seemed to understand this girl's pain and made a special effort to be a friend to the child.

You are your child's teacher in the realm of emotions, and as you read together, you will encounter stories about love, anger, kindness, sadness, guilt, pity, and more. You can naturally identify and talk about these, encouraging your child to express his feelings and to talk about what you are reading.

Don't overlook the importance and pleasure of making up your own stories for your children. I noticed that there were times when our children loved my stories and at other times preferred stories from a book. Be sensitive to their age needs and preferences.

TALKING TOGETHER

It is crucially important that you take the time to talk with your child about difficulties he may be having. This opportunity may come when you are reading together, but it is also likely to happen in moments when you least expect it. As you talk, you hope to discover how your child responds to problems. As you assess where he is, you will be able to help him face the real world of his age-level. You want to teach your child to respond to difficulties in optimistic ways and help him to become a hopeful person.

People who tend to pessimism respond internally in totally different ways than more optimistic people. Excellent research by Morton Seligman and others have shown that there are three important differences between the two types.

Pessimists tend to consider a problem or mishappening as *permanent*—as though the effects will last forever. Second, pessimists see a problem as *pervasive*—as though it will ruin their entire lives. And third, they tend to *blame themselves* for the problem, thus causing guilt and depression.

Optimists do the opposite. They tend to consider mishaps as *temporary* and are able to slough them off and not worry about them. Second, they see problems as *localized*, affecting only a part of their lives. Because they don't dwell on the problems, they can keep their minds on positive thoughts. Third, optimists tend to *blame others* for their problems.[5]

Of course, neither response is always the correct one, and we can't use this research as a fail-safe guide. But I have found it helpful in keeping my own thinking and emotional responses on track, as well as in teaching my children.

Imagine that your daughter goes out for a sport but

doesn't make the team. She comes home in a terrible mood, sulking and behaving irritably. You want her to express her anger verbally, right? Yes, and you can expect it to be unpleasant. You keep yourself calm by knowing what to expect from her and by giving her your example of maintaining control of your anger.

If you handle your daughter well when she expresses anger, she will later want to learn from you how to cope with this and other disappointments. If she is young enough to enjoy reading stories together, you could find one in which a main character suffered disappointment. This could be used to comfort her as well as teach her how to approach similar problems. Then you could talk together about her discouragement and possible approaches to the way she is feeling. What a priceless opportunity to guide your daughter to become strong in hope. Naturally, you want to incorporate your Christian belief in the discussion as well.

As children grow older, you will want to talk more about specific feelings involved in their responses. In the situation just mentioned, you could discuss hurt, pain, disappointment, anger, discouragement, hate, or any other feeling your daughter experienced. One reason for this is to help her verbalize her feelings instead of acting them out behaviorally. The next step is to move her from unpleasantness toward pleasantness.

You will also want to use such situations to help your child handle blame. She will probably want to criticize and blame herself, if she is what I call a 25 percenter. If she is more of a 75 percenter, she will tend to blame someone or something else. It is vital for her to learn whether blame is appropriate and where it should be directed. Far too much blaming is destructive in nature. In our example, your daughter needs to learn that no blame is indicated. Trying out for a team is a risk that takes courage and you are proud of her for doing it. Trying out is an accomplishment in itself.

Even if your daughter does not respond positively to your encouragement, let me assure you that it will have a tremendous effect on her for the rest of her life. She will never forget it and will always be grateful that you cared about her so much.

BEING AVAILABLE TO YOUR CHILDREN

As children enter adolescence, they still need your guidance as much as ever. You will want to make yourself available to them, and also structure times when the normal adolescent defenses are down. This can best be done when both parent and teenager are relaxed and nonpressured. Nonpressured time is time when neither parent nor child feels the need to say or do anything. Examples of such times are when you are waiting in line together, eating in a slow restaurant, riding in a car, or watching television. At such times, teenagers feel free to relax, be themselves, and share their feelings, hopes, and thoughts with a parent.

You need patience to take advantage of such moments. You also should remember that teenagers are not miniature adults. They are children in transition and have the same basic needs as younger children do.

Of course, the primary quality all children need is unconditional love. But they also need help in *identifying and labeling their feelings*. A primary reason for this is that children often show anger when they are actually experiencing other feelings such as rejection, stress, loneliness, inadequacy, or weakness. When they are feeling bad already, the last thing they need is to have a parent's anger dumped on them. Yet, the child's display of anger could confuse a parent into taking the wrong tack. So, the sooner the child learns to tell the difference between anger and other feelings, the sooner he can express himself in more exact and pleasing ways.

Another approach which may present itself at random moments is one I call *predicting*. Since there are basic problems which provoke anger in the various stages of development, you can prepare your child to handle these situations. For example, school children need to feel that they are part of their peer group. Because of this need, they are extremely sensitive to rejection or criticism, including teasing.

During times with the child, you can use the art of predicting, especially as it applies to social interaction. You can tell your child beforehand about some positive and negative events that will likely happen to him. There are several ways to do this.

My favorite is to make up a story that includes a typical childhood encounter, in which a child is ill-treated by his peers and then learns to cope with it. Of course, I emphasize the positive, because I want the child to look forward to social interchanges, not dread them.

It is often helpful to share your own experiences. While you may not have encountered exactly the same kinds of events, you have surely had similar feelings to what your child is now dealing with, and it is the feeling content of your own experience that will communicate with him.

These natural encounters of availability enable parents to maintain a positive home atmosphere, confident that their children will learn to handle the negative interactions of life. Wise parents provide a safe and warm haven in which they train their children to cope with the harsh realities they will face.

No matter what occurs in the lives of your children, you want them to behave as people of integrity, who tell the truth, keep their promises, and assume responsibility for their own behavior. To develop this way, they need to be prepared for life as it is and can be.

Temptations to behave with less than integrity are everywhere, and rationalizations for unethical and immoral behavior are on the rise. But parents, and grandparents, are in a wonderful position to shape the lives of loved children. As we take advantage of our times alone with them, we can share who we are and what we hope and pray for them. Training a child is a long process, but one we dare not give up on.

HANDLING MISBEHAVIOR

With any child, parents have to expect some episodes that can be labeled as bad behavior. It is helpful when they know how to deal with these in the most effective ways. And so, let's look at some of the most common.

♦ Whining. How do you respond to a child's whining? It can be so irritating that you may need to fight the urge to dump your anger on the child: "Stop that whining right now or you will be punished!"

If you do this, you have lost the battle. When you dump anger on your child, you are giving him more ammunition to use against you. Also, you are letting him know that he really upsets you. Later when he wants to manipulate you by further upsetting you, he will know that whining works. The more you dump anger on the child for whining, the more likely he is to whine.

Also, the more you cast anger on your child, the more you are forcing him to oversuppress his anger and to develop anti-authority and passive-aggressive attitudes and behaviors.

It is possible to dump anger on a child not only by yelling but also by whining back. A parent who does this is unloading hostility as well as providing a poor example of how to manage anger. And, of course, the parent is ridiculing and mimicking the child.

You have several choices in how you will respond to whining and you need to select the ones which work best for you. With most children, simply ignoring the whining will suffice. If this is ineffective, you can talk to the child in a calm, cool tone, "I can't hear you when you talk in that voice. Use your nice voice so I can understand what you want."

Generally, children will respond to this approach, but not always. If they continue to whine, make doubly sure that you remain calm. If you respond emotionally and simply give up, the whining wins.

My favorite approach at such a time is to distract the child by involving him in something fun. If the whining still continues, then I leave him alone in a safe place, and tell him that I will be glad to talk further when he can use his nice voice.

Some children do seem to be natural born whiners. If you have one of these in your home, it is life-saving for you to learn the approaches mentioned above. Their whining will lessen, but the process will be slow and arduous. In extreme cases, you may consider time-outs or positive reinforcement which we will consider later.

♦ Tantrums and Violent Outbursts. Preschool children are especially prone to use temper tantrums as a way of controlling their parents. Various primitive triggers such as tiredness, thirst, hunger, heat, cold, or pain cause the tantrums. At that age, children find it hard to soothe themselves, and they need parents to help them learn to calm themselves and gain control over their behavior.

Temper tantrums are difficult for parents to deal with, especially when they happen in public. The same guidelines given for whining apply here. It is essential that parents remain calm and try to ignore the tantrum. They may need something to occupy their minds, like doing a chore around the house, particularly one that makes a loud background noise.

Usually, ignoring the tantrum without seeming upset will suffice. If the tantrum continues beyond a reasonable time, you can give the child a limit in which to regain control. At the end of this time, you should consider a punishment such as time-out, loss of privilege, or extra chores.

The parent's calmness shows the child that the parent is in firm control and will not be influenced by the tantrum. Something that helps many parents to keep themselves calm is to hum, sing, or think about pleasant memories or happy plans for the future. The singing or humming may soothe the child.

In school-age children, other factors that trigger anger are rejection and criticism by peers, insecurity in their parents' love, or judgments that seem unfair.

Deep muscle relaxation is a technique that aids children in calming down when they are angry. You need to teach this when they and you are feeling relaxed and happy so that they can then apply the technique when they are feeling tense or out of control. You teach the child to tense and then relax each body part—left foot, left leg, right foot, right leg, etc. It often works well to have the child imagine a favorite comic character doing the exercise at the same time.

As my children grew older, I selected a certain sign or word to link to relaxation. I could then use that sign or word as a signal when I saw that they were becoming upset. This helped them prevent increased anger on many occasions. The sign I used was to place my right index finger next to my nose and then suddenly move it forward. The signal I used was, "Cool it," said in a soft tone. Incidentally, if I started to get upset or tense, I would tell myself, "I think I had better cool it."

_____

COMMUNICATION

Thomas Gordon, author of *Parent Effectiveness Training*, has long advocated the use of "I" messages rather than "you" messages. As parents use "I" messages, they are training their children to express feelings, including anger, without developing the destructive habit of blaming.[6]

For example, a teenager has forgotten to leave his muddy boots outside and walks inside the house, dirtying the floor and carpets. If a parent says, "Now look what you've done!" the statement is going to provoke anger and tension. The parent could say, "I feel upset when mud is brought into the house." That statement may seem almost too calm, but because it is said in a calmer tone than the first one, and because it lays no direct blame, it will cause less tension. And the real payoff comes when the teenager begins to use "I" messages. "I" statements go a long ways in teaching children to take responsibility for their own behavior.

Silence is a vital part of communication, and it can take many forms in the family. One of the most important uses of silence is the time spent calming down after there has been tension or anger between family members. Meg Eastman comments on this, "When you and/or your child are highly charged, trying to discuss what's wrong might make you both feel angrier and more frustrated."

Ms. Eastman also points out another value of silence, during those times when children want to contest with parents about nonnegotiable rules. Although there is really no point in discussing things that are already settled, the hardest task for most parents is to just be quiet.[7]

SETTING LIMITS

In any home, some behavior problems are going to lead to a need for further limits and, at times, punishment. When a child is out of control, being defiant, or challenging parental authority, we must use appropriate means of control.

Parents have five ways to control a child. Two are positive, two are negative, and one is neutral. They are:

Positive: Requests and Gentle Physical Manipulation.

Negative: Commands and Punishment.

Neutral: Behavior Modification.

The effectiveness of any of these is going to depend on how well we are keeping our children's emotional tanks full.

We certainly should use *requests* whenever we can,

because they are positive and can calm anger. Requests are questions, "Would you do that for me?" Requests give strong, positive, nonverbal messages, such as, "I respect you as a person. I also respect the fact that you have feelings and opinions. I expect you to take responsibility for your behavior."

I wish requests always worked, but they don't. This means that sometimes we must use *commands*. Because a command is an imperative statement and carries a negative connotation, it may elicit anger. It seems to convey, "I don't care that you have feelings or opinions about this and I am not concerned about your taking responsibility for your own behavior. I simply expect you to do what I say. In fact, I am taking responsibility for your behavior."

Gentle physical manipulation is a positive way to control a child's behavior. This works especially well with young children, as when you lead a toddler away from a hot stove or toward a kind of play that will be more acceptable.

Punishment is the second negative form of behavior control. Unfortunately, when they see misbehavior, most parents assume that punishment should be used. They are caught by what I call the "punishment trap." Parents who use punishment as the primary way of disciplining a child or teenager will provoke great amounts of needless anger in the child. They will also force the child to oversuppress anger and develop passive-aggressive attitudes and behavior. This is especially dangerous if the parents are angry when they use punishment.

Yes, we must occasionally use punishment, but we need to use it wisely and carefully. And we can avoid many problems associated with punishment by planning ahead. I recommend sitting down with your spouse or a good friend and planning the appropriate punishment for an offense. You know how obsessed children are with being "fair." The punishment must fit the crime. A child knows when a parent is being too harsh or too lenient. When the time comes that a punishment is warranted, you will already have your response ready. This kind of planning will keep your own anger from irrationally influencing your behavior, and your child will be grateful.

TIME-OUT

Every parent should be familiar with time-out. This is simply to have the child stand or sit in a specified place for a certain length of time. It can be quite effective when a child's anger is out of control. The widely accepted length of time is one minute for every year of a child's age.

If your child is calm after that time, praise him. If he remains out of control, tell him that he can discontinue the time-out when he has regained his self-control. If your child is destructive to the room or objects in it, find a place you know is childproof, with only a few of the child's toys or books. Time-outs are usually the first punishment to use for anger or rageous behavior.

LOSS OF PRIVILEGE AND RESTRICTIONS

Every child has a favorite TV program or play activity. If a time-out doesn't work, the loss of a privilege may be an effective punishment. I have seen many children who simply could not tolerate the idea of missing a TV show and who respond to this much more than to a time-out.

Restrictions are more appropriate to older children and teenagers. But if they are used too often, they may back-fire on you, especially if you forget what you said or later find that the restrictions you set are unenforceable. When this happens, you greatly undermine your control of the house-hold and lessen your children's respect for you.

You'll want to use restrictions frugally, making sure the situation is important enough to justify the penalty. If used sparingly and wisely, restrictions are extremely effective in training children.

COMPENSATION AND CHORES

If a child has caused hurt or loss to another person, you certainly need to consider having him make compensation or restitution. This should, of course, be appropriate to the child's age and ability to repay or make a sacrifice. Also, an apology is in order. Compensation is sometimes difficult to assess, and you may need to consult others to determine a fair amount.

Doing extra chores can be an effective means of rein-forcing the consequences of misbehavior. If you use this method, be sure the time and number and difficulty of chores are appropriate to the child and also to the offense.

BEHAVIOR MODIFICATION

Behavior modification has its place in childrearing. However, it is a mistake to use it as a primary way to relate to a child.

Behavior modification is a system that uses *positive reinforcement*—interjecting a positive commodity into a child's environment; *negative reinforcement*—withdrawing a positive commodity from a child's environment; and *punishment*—interjecting a negative commodity into a child's environment.

An example of positive reinforcement is to reward a child's good behavior by giving him a treat. A negative reinforcement is to withhold valued privileges, such as a television program, for inappropriate behavior. An example of punishment, sometimes called aversion technique, is to pinch the child on the trapezius for inappropriate behavior.

My objection to using behavior modification as the primary way of relating to a child is that many parents substitute this for emotional nurturance. When they overuse this technique, the child does not feel sufficiently loved.

Another problem with overusing behavior modification is that the child will develop a disturbed value system, as he learns to do what is expected of him for a reward. Over time, he will develop an attitude of "What's in it for me?"

Wise parents use behavior modification sparingly. Some of the discipline techniques already discussed, such as time-outs, fall into this category. Behavior modification tends to be formal and impersonal, and should generally be used for specific, recurring behavioral problems for which the child is neither sorry nor defiant.

A situation in which this works well is when siblings fight with each other. When our boys were five and nine, they frequently fought, and our requests to stop had effect for only a few hours. Punishments also had brief effect and were unpleasant for everyone. But what did work was a reward system, a chart with stars—one star for every minute of peace, gradually increasing the time intervals until the fighting stopped. We gave each boy an appropriate reward for a certain number of stars.

One word of warning about this technique—it takes time, consistency, real effort, and patience. Don't start it unless you are prepared to stay with it. Otherwise, it will fail.

In all aspects of relationship with your children, you want to emphasize the positive whenever possible. When you do this, you will be more effective in discipline when it is necessary, and also in total training of your children, including teaching them to handle anger.

The most powerful "positive reinforcers" are the everyday, natural, nonverbal ways you give approval, such as listening attentively to a child, giving smiles, hugs, and spending time with the child. These natural ways of motivating a child are not part of the behavior modification model, and they go much further in helping you achieve the kind of family life you desire.

T E N

Innate Responses to Authority

In the chapters you've already read, you have seen some references to 75 percenters and 25 percenters. Now I want to explain what that is.

In my psychiatric practice over the past twenty-five years, I have observed that most people tend to respond to authority in one of two ways. They lean toward being either pro-authority or anti-authority. It has seemed to me that the pro-group is about 25 percent of the population and the anti-group about 75 percent. And, of course, some people lean more strongly than others.

I believe the best way to understand this distribution is by the graph, Attitudes Toward Authority, which you will find at the end of this chapter. As you can see, the pro-authority 25 percenters and the anti-authority 75 percenters are each on their own bell curve. A 25 percenter can be mild, moderate, or extreme, just as a 75 percenter can be anywhere from mildly anti-authority to extremely anti-authority. Everyone has a basic attitude toward authority which is present at birth as a personality trait. This attitude toward authority can be somewhat modified by a child's upbringing and environment, but the basic trait remains dominant.

These groupings do not connect to the many personality types so much discussed in certain circles today. An extrovert could be either pro or anti, as could an introvert. In both groups we find all kinds of people. So, please do not try to connect my groupings to intuitive, sanguine, choleric, obsessive-compulsive, or whatever labels you use.

How a person responds to almost anything in life depends on one's attitude toward authority, and that attitude depends on this personality trait.

Every child is born with a unique personality that is congenital in nature. At conception, the parents supplied the genetic traits from which the personality developed. Because personality is given, it is not a matter of better or worse, but different. The more we can understand a child's basic nature, the better we can work to enhance and enrich what that child has brought into the world.

To help you better understand the two responses to authority, I want to tell you about each of them, look at a few children who are part of the groups, and then suggest ways that you can best deal with your own children.

TWENTY-FIVE PERCENTERS

Twenty-five percenters are born with a need to be under authority. They want approval and praise. They want someone to tell them what to do and to structure their time for them. You might think that this kind of child would be very easy to raise—you just tell her what to do and she does it. Then you add the praise.

If you think this sounds too simple, you're right.

Twenty-five percenters are as difficult to raise as 75 percenters, because they must be taught to think for themselves, to stand on their own two feet, and stop depending so much on others.

Twenty-five percenters are easily controlled by guilt since they are so prone to it. Most parents of children in this group control them in exactly this way without realizing it and then take great pride in the fact that they have such wonderfully disciplined children.

Julie is the oldest of five children. She is a quiet and obedient girl whose parents, Evelyn and Richard, are controlling her by subtle guilt.

When a friend invited Julie to a swimming party, she asked her mother who replied, "Oh, I'm sorry, Julie. I had planned to meet your father for dinner downtown. I was hoping you could watch your brothers and sisters for me. Oh, well, never mind. I'll do it another time."

Although Julie knew her mother rarely got out of the house, she really wanted to go to the swimming party. However, she would have felt terrible being the one to keep her mom from some needed time away. "Go ahead, Mom. My swimsuit is faded anyway. I'd rather wait until I get a new one before I go to a swimming party. You go on and meet Daddy for dinner."

It became easier for Evelyn to ask Julie to stay with the children, because Julie never complained. In fact, she was so convincing that her mother thought she actually enjoyed it. And she did, once in a while, but many times she would have liked to be with her friends. It was guilt that kept her home.

When 25 percenters are very young, they are so easy to manage. Their parents are often overheard telling other parents, "If you would just be more firm with your child, she would be like Julie." But there is really no way to compare the two types, and many children are damaged by parents who think that all children can be raised in the same manner.

When parents control their children with guilt, they are controlling them in the worst possible way. Twenty-five percenters are so eager to please that they are easily crushed. They take everything too personally and seriously. They are also afraid that they are going to hurt someone or do something wrong. Because they can be perfectionistic, they want to do everything exactly right. A little bit of criticism can smash their egos and make them feel so guilty that they cannot develop into their own persons.

Most parents of such children don't see this. They just enjoy having a nice child who always does exactly what he is told to do and never gives anyone a hard time. What these parents fail to realize is that their children are keeping all their feelings to themselves. As perfectionists, they are very self-critical. They don't expect everything to be perfect, but they expect everything to be much better than they can make it.

Twenty-five percenters have such high expectations that each day can be a disappointment. Even if every event in a day is good but one, they will see only that one. Therefore, they are prone to depression.

Brett is a sophomore in high school. On this particular day, he made an A on a math test, an A on an English quiz, and got a book report back with yet another A. What a great day! That afternoon, he hit a home run which scored the winning point for his team.

When he got home from school, he found a note from his mom saying she would be late. That was fine with

Brett, since he was on his way to the bowling alley. He went to his closet and reached for his red bowling shirt, but it wasn't there. He discovered it in the laundry basket, with dark stains on it.

Now Brett's day was ruined. His team was bowling in a tournament and he didn't have a shirt! Everything good about his day left him.

Brett's story illustrates the way a 25 percenter thinks. He can easily become depressed over an insignificant happening, and depression causes anger. Because he wants above all to please, he keeps that anger inside, causing even deeper depression. This in turn causes more anger, which the child directs inward toward himself.

This kind of child can suffer from years of guilt manipulation, when his parents are not aware of what is happening inside of him. He has not been taught to think for himself or to express his feelings verbally. As a consequence, he is on his way toward becoming a depressed and angry adult.

The natural need of all humans to be loved and to feel self-worth is multiplied in the 25 percenter. When his parents do not realize his low self-esteem and unintentionally leave him with an empty emotional tank, he goes outside his home for need satisfaction. By the time he is a teenager, he may be involved in destructive behavior.

SEVENTY-FIVE PERCENTERS

Pat and I have two sons. Dale is our 25 percenter who was born asking, "Dad, is there anything you and Mom would like me to do for you?"

David arrived in the world with an order that could

be heard by everyone in shouting distance, "Would you people please step out of the way? I have a life to live, and I would like to get on with it with as little interference as possible!"

David was one of those "I'd rather do it myself" kids, and there was never any doubt about how he was feeling. These children want to do their own thinking and make their own decisions. They can become angry when anyone tells them what to do. They want to learn things on their own.

On the surface, 75 percenters may seem much harder to raise, but this is not really so. Even though they are born with an anti-authority attitude, they take about the same amount of patience, love, and understanding as their more compliant siblings.

The drive to think for themselves gives the 75 percenters a natural talent for leadership. And I find it easier to keep this kind of child under control than to teach the 25 percenter how to think for himself. However, this child is likely to become angry when you are trying to train and discipline him.

When our David was nearly fourteen, he announced one Sunday morning, "I'm not going to church today."

"Oh, come on, David," I replied, "you know that you have a good time, once you're there."

He gave in and went with us, and didn't say any more about it for a few weeks. And then, out of the blue he announced, "I'm not going to church today. I told you before that I didn't want to go, and I'm not going."

This time I could see that it was useless to talk with him more—he was so determined that forcing him would have created an anti-church attitude that could have been difficult to reverse. I wanted to handle this without alienating David, so that we could keep him on the road to maturity.

"Do you like Sunday School?" I asked.

"Yeah, I don't mind Sunday School."

"OK, I'll tell you what we'll do. You go to Sunday School and then your mother or I will drive you home and stay here with you during church."

David agreed to this. Knowing that he was a 75 percenter, Pat and I wanted to prevent the anger toward spiritual things which can develop when these matters are forced. David was naturally anti-authority, and so we chose for the moment not to pressure him. We didn't feel that we were being permissive; rather, that we had a plan. David knew how we believed and was just testing us.

After this arrangement went on for four or five weeks, I could tell that it was getting old for David. And he knew that Pat and I were suffering because of it. We wanted to be in church together. Finally he said, "Oh, all right, I'll go to church for your sakes." And that was that.

Now, I can't promise this strategy will work for all 75 percenters. It depends a great deal on the kind of overall relationship you have with your child. The key to handling this type of child is to keep things positive and not become too authoritarian, particularly in relationship to spiritual matters. The statistics are a bit hazy on the number of children raised in the church who leave when they are grown. However, whatever the actual numbers, they aren't good, as we can all attest from cases we have observed in our own churches and communities.

PASSIVE AGGRESSION AND 25/75

In chapter 6, we talked about the one "normal" period of passive aggression we will encounter with our children, the early teen stage. Remember that passive-aggressive behavior goes for the jugular. In most homes, one of the top priorities is for the children to do well in school. Therefore, this is one of the main areas in which passive aggression shows itself. Whatever is most important to the parents is where it will crop up.

When 75 percenters begin to do poorly in school, it is well for the parents not to make a big deal out of it. The bigger the issue, the more the child is going to continue the behavior. After all, as long as the parents and teachers are taking responsibility for the grades, why should the teenager? Our older son, David, was an extreme 75 percenter whose grades dropped dramatically in eighth and ninth grade. But, as I related in an earlier chapter, he was able to right the situation himself when he realized he wouldn't make it into a competitive college unless he changed his ways.

Dale, our 25 percenter, never wavered in his approach to schoolwork. He wanted to please and continued to make excellent grades all through high school.

Thirteen- to fifteen-year-olds are unconsciously and sometimes consciously against almost everything. This is especially true of the 75 percenters who are angry most of the time. What we need to do is to keep the anger coming out of their mouths instead of allowing it to stay inside.

This is very difficult for parents, because their natural inclination is to quiet their teenagers, suppress their anger, and keep peace in the house. But sometimes I have to ask the parents I counsel, "Would you rather have a son yelling at you or a son overdosed on drugs? Would you rather have daughter harping and screaming or a pregnant daughter?"

Of course, the answer is "Neither," but this is seldom possible. How many times I have observed wonderful parents in agony when they have discovered that their well-behaved and polite teenager is pregnant, on drugs, or having some other devastating problem. Please remember that unpleasant verbalization of anger is only temporary if we do our jobs in training our children in managing their anger. Some of my most wonderful experiences were in seeing my children make progress in expressing their anger verbally and pleasantly.

I always tell parents to remove the pressure from their younger teens by allowing them to verbalize their anger, and then to respond to them in a mature way. This is *not* being overly permissive as long as we are handling our children's anger appropriately and leading them up the Anger Ladder. Suppressing anger is something like depressing an inflated balloon with a bulge in it. If you push the bulge in, it is going to come out somewhere else. If you try to keep your children from expressing anger, you can be sure it will pop out in another area of their lives.

In passive-aggressive behavior, a teenager gets rid of anger by upsetting his parents. So whatever upsets parents most is what the kid goes for. What would upset Christian parents the most? Rebellion against spirituality, of course. So, where is the kid's behavior going to be targeted? Against the church and devotional practices. But this is no guarantee that other family priorities will escape notice. Parents will probably have to deal with rebellion against their top two or three values.

DENISE AND BILL

Many families are likely to have both a 25 percenter and a 75 percenter, and this can present a challenge. The siblings may experience real tension in getting along with each other and the parents may tend to favor one over the other, in their lack of understanding of what motivates the children.

Tall and slender Denise was a nursing student who came to talk with me. For a while she sat fidgeting and wearing a depressed expression on her face, as she tried to decide what to say. Then she suddenly blurted out, "I'm anorexic, Dr. Campbell. I attended a lecture on anorexia and it made me realize that I am anorexic and bulemic."

Denise began to cry. "I don't want to tell my parents, because they don't think I've done much of anything right in my life as it is. Now they'll be sure to hate me."

I looked into her tear-filled brown eyes. "What are you doing that makes you think you are anorexic, Denise?"

"Well, I starve myself for as long as I can stand it. Then I eat everything in sight, take a laxative, and purge."

"How long have you been doing this?"

"About four months."

I was glad that Denise had recognized her problem early enough that she had not yet reached the point of physical damage. I felt there was a good chance of helping her through this. What we needed to discover was why she felt so negative about herself.

As I began to counsel Denise, her problem unfolded. Her older brother, Bill, was outgoing and aggressive. Denise was the quiet one. Seventy-five and 25.

"Ever since I can remember, Bill had Mom and Dad's attention about something. When he was seven, he developed a life-threatening illness. I stayed with my grandparents while he was in the hospital. I was very lonesome, but hated to bother Mom and Dad because they were upset about Bill.

"When he came home from the hospital, he had to stay in bed for a month. I did everything I could to make him happy. I was glad we were all home together, but Mom hardly noticed me. I don't remember feeling that she should notice me, but now I realize how much I missed her attention.

"When Bill and I were ten and eight, Mom and Dad built a new house and we lived through some very hectic months. I remember that Bill and I fought and then were punished by our father. On one of these occasions, Bill took off, but I went back in the house to finish a job Mom had asked me to do."

Denise told me that she almost always gave in — not just to her brother and parents, but to anyone who crossed her. However, when she entered high school, she began to change.

"I still tried to keep peace at home, but I was a real character at school. In my junior year, I dated a boy who didn't amount to anything. He was just plain trouble. When my folks found out I was seeing him, they lectured me for two weeks. I never went out with him again.

"I always felt guilty if I did something that displeased my parents, and thought I was probably the worst person in the world."

In her second year of college, Denise's grades went from respectable to failing, because she skipped so many classes. She kept her grades from her parents for a while, until her mother made a surprise visit to campus and Denise had to tell her the truth. Her parents moved her home and informed her that she would have to get a job and pay them back for the money she had wasted on education, or lack thereof.

"I held two or three different jobs, finally succeeding in paying back the money, but feeling worse and worse about myself. I had no particular direction, and never completed anything I started.

"All this time, Mom was directing my life. Since I didn't think she had done such a great job with her own life, I resented her interference in mine. But I couldn't afford to move and so had to put up with her interference. When I told her that I was going to finish my education, she seemed pleased and offered to loan me the money but I refused. I knew I would have to do something on my own soon, or I never would. So I borrowed the money and moved out of my parents' home and started back to school.

"I fell into the same trap of trying to settle everyone's arguments. I felt I was always there for other people, but they never seemed to be there for me. As time for graduation drew near, I panicked. I had never completed anything of importance and was afraid I wouldn't finish this either.

"I had always been slightly overweight, or so I thought, and so I started on a diet about the same time I panicked about graduation. When I discovered I could lose weight easily, I felt I was doing something right at last. But the weight loss became an obsession."

After several weeks of intensive counseling, Denise began to understand that she was a 25 percenter. She also came to realize that her parents had not interacted with her in ways that would meet her needs. They had always loved her, and didn't know that her quiet ways were deceiving. Because she didn't demand extra attention, she didn't get any. Her parents just assumed that her emotional tank was full, and they tended instead to the obvious demands of Bill, a classic 75 percenter.

Fortunately, Denise's story has a happy ending. She graduated third in her class and is now working in a large hospital. She and her parents have a real relationship at last, based on love and understanding. Her parents now realize that she needs attention from them, even if she is quiet.

Do you see how easy it was for Denise's parents to control her? She wanted approval and praise, and tried to be the perfect little girl. But this finally became more than she could handle. Her lack of emotional fulfillment resulted in anger and frustration which turned inward and then manifested itself as anorexia and bulimia.

And what about Denise's spirituality? As an adolescent, she attended church and made a profession of faith. She became the exemplary teenager — until her junior year of high school when she rejected her spiritual training, considering it "baby stuff." However, she continued to attend church because she wanted her parents' approval.

Denise did, however, continue to feel a deep need for God. She was gradually drawn to prayer and Bible reading on her own, but avoided church activities. Like most 25 percenters, she did not believe her thoughts and decisions were as important as those of more assertive persons. As she came to understand that her intelligence, thought processes, and decision-making were as effective and legitimate as those of other people, she gradually learned to depend on herself and her own opinions with confidence. She was then more secure in groups, including the church.

We need to be very careful that we provide the nurture our 25 percenters need, in spirit and emotion, body and mind. Because they, like Denise, are not demanding, and because their siblings may be like Bill, always demanding the attention of parents, it is easy to have a family life that is very out of balance. We want all of our children to grow into strong and healthy and responsible adults.

BACK TO OUR 75 PERCENTERS

Our 75 percenters differ from their more cautious siblings in another important way. They tend to be more global and general in their thinking, while the 25 percenters are more focused on specific detail. This means that the two types reach conclusions in different ways.

I am a 25 percenter and my older son, David, is a 75 percenter. He and I perceive situations in our own ways and have had to learn to appreciate the perspective of the other. Often I have come to the conclusion that he has the better way of handling problems than I do.

When David was twenty years old, he and I decided to go scuba diving in another country. On our arrival, we found that our baggage was missing. I didn't think too much about it until we realized that it was in plain sight in an airport official's office. When we brought this to the attention of the authorities, they initially denied that it was our luggage. When we insisted that it was indeed ours, they said they had no key for that office. David and I waited several hours while they "looked for" the key. As they continued to ignore our inquiries, my anger mushroomed until I was ready to explode. Complicating the whole thing for me was that their attitudes were all too reminiscent of some prejudicial ways I had been treated as a child.

David knows me pretty well, and he could see that I was about to verbally attack the officials and possibly get myself in trouble — or at least give them another excuse to hold our luggage. The training I had given David in handling anger came to fruition as he took over and said, "Dad, you are too upset. Sit down and I'll handle this." I gladly sat down and kept my mouth shut while David kept his cool, handled it beautifully, and got our luggage back.

As a 25 percenter, I focused too much on one detail—the way we were being treated—and I overreacted to that. David, on the other hand, saw the whole picture and could keep his perspective. We were in a foreign land where the customs differed from ours. He also maintained that this was simply an inconvenience and did not need to interfere with the wonderful trip we had planned.

In this case, the basic 75-percenter tendencies prevailed. But, in other situations, 25-percenter traits work out best. How fortunate for the person who has learned how and when to use his strengths and when to let other people take over.

Seventy-five percenters do not always feel high respect for 25 percenters. Because the latter are more sensitive, feel deeply, and are more easily hurt, the 75 percenters usually consider them as weak, fragile, and easily intimidated. However, they tend to be less sensitive and also less prone to empathy and understanding of another's view. It is easy for a 75 percenter to become calloused, uncaring, selfish—and even a sociopath.

As parents of this type of children, we must not only keep their emotional tanks full so that they understand love and care, but also teach them empathy and sympathy. And, of course, we need to train them to handle their anger in a mature fashion. A strong 75 percenter who is not well loved, who has never learned to understand and respect others, and who has become even more anti-authority with passive-aggressive behavior, will most likely develop a sociopathic personality.

Because these children are less sensitive and tend to blame other people, they may have difficulty in experiencing guilt. And a certain amount of guilt is necessary for the development of a normal conscience.

As parents we want to be sure that we don't weaken the guilt they may feel. The most effective way to wipe away guilt is through punishment. When a child feels genuinely guilty about misbehaving, punishment and especially corporal punishment will wipe it away as clean as a slate. This is one of the reasons that punishment must be used wisely and sparingly. Punishment should *never* be used when a child feels genuinely sorry for misbehavior. If it is, it will prevent the child from developing a normal conscience, and nothing is more prevalent today than lack of conscience. One main cause is overuse of punishment when there has been too little unconditional love. The result of this punishment trap is an increasing number of sociopaths.

But our 75 percenters are our natural leaders. We need for them to care about their fellow citizens with understanding and good conscience.

We parents are in a wonderful position to truly leave this world a better place than we found it. A well-equipped 75 percenter is a rare delight. That is, a caring, unselfish 75 percenter of good conscience who has developed into a leader motivated for the common good and not just his own glory. What a worthwhile goal for us as parents to help these children grow into true leaders.

ATTITUDES TOWARD AUTHORITY

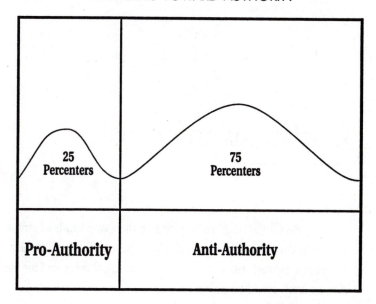

ELEVEN

Christians and Anger

As Christians, we experience the same kinds of stress and pain that non-Christians do. We share with them similar losses and privations, as well as some personal fears and memories we wish could be different.

As believers in Jesus Christ, we know that we are supposed to be different in some respects, and we hope that we are different in our responses and intentions. And sometimes, we are even tempted to believe that the "all things made new" is actually finished, inside and outside of us. But we frequently have to admit that we are very much still in process, and that the promise of completion isn't until the "Day of Jesus Christ."

Those of us who have been Christians for many years should be able to avoid many anger-producing behaviors. We have the words of Holy Scripture and support from the church, and we know in most situations how God wants us to behave.

However, within the Christian community, we find certain aspects of life and belief that actually intensify anger, and then lead people to suppress rather than deal with it.

In this chapter, we are going to look at the place where Christians come together — the church — and at two evils which directly threaten the well-being and ministry of both clergy and lay people as they seek to serve God—passive-aggressive anger and sociopathic attitudes and behaviors.

RESPONSES TO AUTHORITY

You'll remember that in chapter 10 we talked about 25 and 75 percenters and how they differ in their responses to authority. From my observation, I believe about three fourths of the population is innately anti-authority in orientation, although not necessarily in behavior. However, we don't find that kind of mix everywhere we go. An extreme example of imbalance is a prison, where we would find a higher percentage of anti-authority individuals.

Because 25 percenters are already such a minority, it seems unlikely that they would be a majority in very many places. However, this is just the situation we find far too often in a place where it ought not to be—the church.

Twenty-five percenters, as you will remember, are wonderful people. But they want and need to be under authority, and many of them have not learned sufficiently to think for themselves. While at first glance this need to be under authority might seem to be desirable, it does not work to the advantage of the local church or the kingdom of God. Nor does it reflect biblical teachings. Christ's words about being under authority are not just for those who have a need to be so, but for all people, including those who have had to learn through difficult experience that they too must be under authority.

Seventy-five percenters who have reached a significant level of Christian maturity are desperately needed by the church. We need them in the pews, for they bring a healthy—and biblical—skepticism to church with them. If they have learned how to deal with their own anti-authority attitudes and anger, and if they are reaching for Christian maturity, they are the very ones who can maintain a stable balance in the church in times of stress or disagreement. They are the ones who can prevent power-hungry people from taking control and advantage of the congregation. Mature 75 percenters can provide the sensible leadership so needed in our congregations.

We see these people using their talents in the business and professional world, as well as in government. So why are they so conspicuously absent from the church? And why are some Christians who regularly attend church not using their gifts in ministry?

There is no single answer to these questions. However, we do know that some people are repelled by the attitudes they hear expressed from certain church leaders, and we also know that certain groups of Christians are discouraged or prevented from using their real abilities. One such group that is excluded from meaningful service in many churches is women. While I don't wish to discuss ordination, I know that there are hundreds of creative ways women can serve God in and through the church, that do not require ordination or licensing. And yet, in far too many places, women have been relegated to the kitchen and the nursery. Of course, I believe that teaching young children is one of the most important responsibilities of the church, one that should be given only to the most qualified and Christlike members. But then, my opinion is not shared by most church leaders.

When a church does not have a natural balance of people and is lacking those who could offer gifted leadership, it is prone to more anger rather than less, because it becomes mired in situations that no one can solve and in feelings that are not resolved. Also, when people are not allowed to use their God-given abilities, they tend to feel resentful at the organization that talks about gifts and then prevents their use.

CONFUSION ABOUT ANGER

Even though we see multiple examples of anger in the Bible, and though there is no suggestion there that people will not get angry, many Christian people seem to interpret the Bible that way. And they do have reasons for this, verses such as Psalm 37:8 which says, "Refrain from anger and turn from wrath."

Most Christians I have known believe that anger is sinful. When they experience normal anger, two things happen. First, they think that they are displeasing God and so they feel guilty. This guilt lowers their self-esteem, causing them to feel unworthy. Many Christians are prone to some depression, because of specific personality traits. Over time, this depression can deepen and be the cause of more anger.

This increasing degree of anger results in the second consequence—the oversuppression of anger. As these people suppress more and more anger, their subconscious minds must find a way to deal with it and find an outlet. The most common outlet is passive-aggressive attitudes and behavior. As we have already seen, passive-aggressive behavior targets people in authority, who often have nothing to do with the actual cause of the anger.

So, here we are in church with people who have

denied their anger and then stuffed it until it has festered into passive-aggressive attitudes against authority. Who is the likely target when this subconscious anger begins to express itself? You're right—the pastor.

PASTORS AT RISK

The ministry has become one of the most stressful of all occupations. Because we live in such an anti-authority society, Christians also have picked up these attitudes and behaviors. One unique way of expressing them is the manner in which we relate to our pastors. They are highly visible authority figures and, as such, are natural targets for passive-aggressive manifestations of anger.

This problem does not diminish over time, because the longer passive-aggressive people know a pastor, the worse will be their attitude and behavior. In such a situation, no matter what the pastor does or doesn't do, he can't escape the increasing, underlying resentment, resistance, and attacks from those to whom he is trying to minister.

I have counseled with many ministers who have been crushed by this phenomenon. And parishioners who may have no part in the angry behaviors tend not to assume responsibility for this tragedy, but rationalize the behaviors of their angry co-members.

John Keaton was the pastor of a church my family and I attended years ago. He was a genuinely good person who had been at the church for seventeen years, and we had come to know him and his family intimately. He was a totally unselfish man, one of the most nonmaterialistic people I have ever met. He had pastored his flock through the ups and downs, joys and sorrows of all those years.

It still seems hard to believe that a prominent member of the congregation, Charles, tormented John for all those years. Charles was well known in the community because he was likable and had a winning way with people. Also, his opinion carried some weight in Christian circles.

I would have thought that Charles would be satisfied with his sphere of influence. And yet, almost daily he criticized John, calling him "liberal," claiming that he did not "preach the Word," and that we should "get rid of him." During all those years, John never retaliated.

Unfortunately, a family with similar opinions joined our church. The husband, Mike, was as vocal as Charles in his condemnation, but he went a step further. When he was elected to the church board, he took advantage of his office, talking to other board members about his discontent with John.

Finally, Mike made a proposal to church members with whom he felt he had influence, that the congregation dismiss John at the next business meeting. Of course, Mike didn't inform families who might be loyal to the pastor, as we were. Fortunately, enough of us who understood the situation were able to clarify the issue at the meeting and convince the thinking people of the church that such a move would destroy the church as well as end an outstanding ministry.

John weathered the crisis in a gracious manner and remained at the church for another three years before accepting a call to a church in a different city. I thank God that he was able to withstand the trials of passive-aggressive attitudes and to survive. He is still in the ministry today.

Thousands of clergy are not enduring as well as John did. In their book *Pastors at Risk*, H.B. London, Jr. and Neil B. Wiseman report the results of a 1991 Survey of Pastors done by the Fuller Institute of Church Growth. The statistics are sobering:

90 percent of pastors work more than 46 hours a week
80 percent believed that pastoral ministry affected their families negatively
33 percent said that being in ministry was an outright hazard to their family
75 percent reported a significant stress-related crisis at least once in their ministry
50 percent felt unable to meet the needs of the job
90 percent felt they were inadequately trained to cope with ministry demands
70 percent say they have a lower self-esteem now than when they started out
40 percent reported a serious conflict with a parishioner at least once a month
37 percent confessed having been involved in inappropriate sexual behavior with someone in the church
70 percent do not have someone they consider a close friend.[1]

The surveys indicated that 40 percent of the pastors had contemplated leaving the ministry in the previous three months. They felt caught in a swirl of an increasingly complex kind of work that places more emphasis on numbers and administration than on spiritual values.

Contemporary spiritual leaders are under a twofold assault—one within and one without.

On the inside of the church, many believers have succumbed to the snares of secularism. Pastors deal daily with diluted dedication, family disintegration, superficial commitments, and an accepted churchly consumerism no longer interested in sacrifice, suffering, or servanthood. Well-worn, friendly old words are still used, but the new meanings refer to a Jesus who provides comfortable happiness and makes no demand on conduct or money. Without our realizing it, the enemy has secularized the church without a shot being fired by anyone.

Outside the church, pastors face a new dark age where the masses have no Christian memory, success is king, and faith issues are far down the average person's priority list after the PTA meeting, latest video release, Little League game, or weekend diversion. The secular masses simply do not see the point. Even though they are sometimes magnanimous toward pastors, they really think ministers are wasting their lives for an absurd cause.[2]

One unique reason that pastors are touched by the anger of parishioners is that some members are extraordinarily "conscientious." Does that sound strange? We need to remember that personality traits may be positive in some situations and negative in others. Conscientiousness is usually positive. But, if it is misguided, it can be destructive.

Conscientiousness becomes misguided when it is contaminated with ambitiousness or anti-authority attitudes and behavior. When this happens a parishioner can misuse his desire to serve God by placing himself above the authority figure, the pastor, and undermining the ministries of the pastor and the church. Because this is increasingly common today, we need mature, clear-thinking Christians who can keep the basic ministries of the church free from the interference of "overly conscientious" (passive-aggressive) Christians.

Do you remember when the disciples James and John came to Jesus to ask for a special favor? When He inquired what they wanted Him to do, they replied:

> "Let one of us sit at Your right and the other at Your left in Your glory."
>
> "You don't know what you are asking," Jesus said. "Can you drink the cup I drink or be baptized with

the baptism I am baptized with?"

"We can," they answered.

Jesus said to them, "You will drink the cup I drink and be baptized with the baptism I am baptized with, but to sit at My right or left is not for Me to grant. These places belong to those for whom they have been prepared."

When the ten heard about this, they became indignant with James and John. Jesus called them together and said, "You know that those who are regarded as rulers of the Gentiles lord it over them, and their high officials exercise authority over them. Not so with you. Instead, whoever wants to become great among you must be your servant, and whoever wants to be first must be slave of all. For even the Son of Man did not come to be served, but to serve, and to give His life as a ransom for many" (Mark 10:37-45).

Isn't that classic? James and John, the Sons of Thunder, or anger, were so "conscientious" that they wanted to be more "spiritual" than the other disciples. That is exactly what Charles and Mike did. In trying to be "conscientious Christians," they wanted to be more "spiritual" by placing themselves above the pastor.

Tragically, pastors who genuinely attempt to *minister* are the most susceptible to poor treatment from their parishioners. Why? Because it is easy to criticize and take advantage of pastors who are sensitive, caring, and unpretentious.

This is not the type we see on television or hear on the radio, and it takes little talent to compare our own pastors with the public preachers who have "magnetic" personalities. Also, we know our pastors and their families all too well—including their blemishes. As Christ said, "Only in his hometown . . . is a prophet without honor" (Mark 6:4).

SOCIOPATHS IN THE SHEEPFOLD

The unavoidable comparison between our pastors and public ministers does not mean that the more public ones are all striving for their own self-exaltation. But some are.

The mass-media religious phenomenon has undermined the church and provided platforms for people I call sociopaths because of their behavior. A sociopath has a natural ability to win the respect, love, and obedience of certain types of people, especially 25 percenters, who tend to avoid thinking for themselves. They are subconsciously looking for a strong and dynamic person to follow, to do their thinking, make their decisions, and to be their leader. Then they can please the leader, and win the praise and approval they crave.

Sociopaths are difficult to describe with precision. It is easier to point to extreme examples that we can all identify. But to do so might be more confusing, especially since I am not that concerned about the extreme sociopath. Many of us who study current happenings in the church are deeply concerned about the more subtle sociopaths. By subtle I mean that on the surface their sociopathic traits are difficult to recognize.

Sociopaths know what is right, but they don't really care. They lack conscience and experience little or no remorse, anxiety, or guilt. The more extreme the sociopathy, the more these persons will actually believe that the wrong they are doing is all right. This is particularly subtle when the underlying purposes of their behavior are wrong, but their behavior seems good *for a time*, before it eventually falls to truth.

The most dangerous sociopath is able not only to behave appropriately, but also to isolate his hearers from sources of information which disagree with what he says publicly. He makes sure that only his "teachings" are heard by Christians. He sets himself up as the "authority" and does not encourage his followers to think for themselves or to test knowledge to see if it is true. He assumes that anyone who disagrees with him must be wrong—even ungodly.

Distortion of truth is becoming increasingly widespread in the body of Christ today. Controlling the knowledge that Christians are exposed to enables the sociopath to mix truth and untruth as he sees fit. He can then manipulate trusting Christians to his own purposes.

Sociopaths strive for money, power, and sometimes sex, usually in that order. The most brilliant ones operate so that they never get caught doing anything wrong. The less brilliant may end up in jail or in disgrace.

Until mass media made religion so lucrative for the entrepreneur, few true sociopaths were drawn into the church or parachurch organizations. But now that a winsome, charming, and manipulative person is able to use the body of Christ for power and wealth, the domination of sociopathy is growing.

Sociopaths may look good on the outside, but their underlying purpose is to use people for their own ends. Among mental health professionals, the sardonic definition of a sociopath is someone whom everybody likes, who gets you to lend him $100, and then makes you feel grateful for the privilege. Does that remind you of anyone? Jesus asked some of those who followed Him:

> Why do you call Me, "Lord, Lord," and do not do what I say? I will show you what he is like who comes to Me and hears My words and puts them into practice. He is like a man building a house, who dug down deep and laid the foundation on rock. When a flood came, the torrent struck

that house but could not shake it, because it was well built. But the one who hears My words and does not put them into practice is like a man who built a house on the ground without a foundation. The moment the torrent struck that house, it collapsed and its destruction was complete (Luke 6:46-49).

I wonder if Jesus was talking about sociopaths. The most troubling aspect of typical sociopaths is that they cannot discern any wrong in what they are doing. They are totally convinced, usually through rationalization, that they are right. They are then able to convince many others that they have a corner on truth. There is certainly nothing wrong with contributing to the pool of knowledge and discerning what is biblically true and what is not. But when these people proclaim that they are the primary bearers of truth, they present a danger for those who follow them and also for the church. Ministries built on sociopathic motivations, especially the acquisition of power, are indeed houses without foundation. Why do they call Christ "Lord" when the foundation on which they build is their own elevation? Yet, some are so cunning, and some Christians so naive, that the leaders are back controlling people even after they have been exposed.

TELLING THE SHEPHERD
FROM THE HIRELING

How can we tell whether a pastor or leader of an organization is a sociopath or a true servant? Many times it is impossible to know for certain, and we should be very cautious in our following and in our condemning. It is usually impossible to understand a person's true character until we have known that person well for at least two years. And it is certain that we cannot know someone simply from a television or radio presentation, or a sermon or two from the pulpit.

Several biblical stories and passages offer us guidance in evaluating those who seek places of leadership. Consider the story of Absalom in the Old Testament as well as the question of James and John. Or, Paul's defense of his own ministry over against others of whom he said, "Such men are false apostles, deceitful workmen, masquerading as apostles of Christ. And no wonder, for Satan himself masquerades as an angel of light. It is not surprising, then, if his servants masquerade as servants of righteousness. Their end will be what their actions deserve" (2 Cor. 11:13-15).

In the Book of Proverbs, we read, "Do not exalt yourself in the king's presence, and do not claim a place among great men; it is better for him to say to you, 'Come up here,' than for him to humiliate you before a nobleman. . . . It is not . . . honorable to seek one's own honor" (25:6-7, 27).

And in Matthew we find the words of Jesus, "For whoever exalts himself will be humbled, and whoever humbles himself will be exalted" (23:12).

One thing is certain: we all need to be very careful of sociopathic persons. Because of poor parenting, as well as the rise in media possibilities, their numbers are increasing. Initially, they may come across as good folks, but as they gain an upper hand, they use people for their own exaltation.

While the tendency toward this evil is as old as mankind, and while we may meet it in any avenue of life, it has gained undue influence in the religious world, as spiritual authority has shifted away from the local congregation to organizations that come to us through the mass media. Many of these "popular" spokespersons are disseminating information that is false, but overlaid with some truth. It is very difficult to distinguish what part is truth and what part is falsehood, and even more difficult to question or confront the person who is speaking.

WHAT IS OUR CHALLENGE?

In a book about children and anger, this chapter might seem a digression from the main point. And yet, I don't think so, since you and your family probably attend a church that has experienced some of the problems we have mentioned, and also because you know the abuses of religion on the wider scale. God's greatest concern is about our character and that should be our concern also, our own character and that of our children, as well as the character of those who influence our families, especially in the church. A great part of character is integrity, and you'll remember that integrity includes telling the truth, keeping promises, and taking responsibility for personal behavior. This standard is for everyone, even "celebrities" and "experts."

We have discussed two destructive forces at work today, passive-aggressive anger which is undermining the ministries of so many local churches, and the sociopathic attitudes and behaviors which increasingly dominate the larger church scene. Both of these evils are the result of poor parenting: passive aggression from the failure to teach children to manage anger in a mature way, and sociopathy from the failure to provide children with adequate nurture and guidance.

To say this is not to condemn parents; they cannot

do the job of parenting alone. Parents need understanding about how to raise their children to be people of integrity who can become mature adults. Most parents don't have enough information and understanding about what their children need.

One reason that I included this difficult and risky chapter is to help parents recognize the dynamics of interaction that may be occurring in a place as important to them and their children as the church. As parents, we want to provide a positive and godly church experience for our children, one that will draw them closer to God and to the kind of life God wants them to live. We want them to become nurturing people who will want to serve more than be served.

WHAT ABOUT THE FUTURE?

Some pages back, we left our 75 percenters and now we want to go back to them, because we need them. Remember, they are indirectly anti-authority, which means that they do not need to be under authority to feel good about themselves. They don't need approval and praise from an authority figure.

These young people are the leaders of the future, and yet they face pitfalls as they are growing up. Those who are strongly influenced by our society, and who also fail to develop mature ways to manage their anger, will become passive aggressive. If they continue to resist authority, they will probably leave the church.

And yet, they *can* develop strong leadership abilities, and also be able to hold their own in conflicts. A clear-thinking 75 percenter of sound Christian character, who handles anger well and who is able to differentiate a genuinely caring ministry from a sociopathic one, is a rare bird indeed. We desperately need this type of person in the church today.

And for all our children, we hope and pray that they will become clear-minded thinkers who are able to make sound decisions and to handle their anger maturely. We want our children to be able to discern between legitimate, accountable, spiritual authority, and that bogus authority which seeks its own gratification without being accountable to anyone. Only then will the church be the haven of hope, rest, renewal, and worship, and have the spiritual influence Christ intends for it to have in society.

I pray that every child will have a church home that is a warm and positive place in which to thrive and grow in the knowledge of God.

TWELVE

Children with Special Problems

With a small percentage of children, nothing seems to work. Parents and teachers can do everything right and still end up with "problem children" on their hands. In recent decades, we have discovered much more about certain kinds of disabilities that can severely handicap children and cause chaos in the home and classroom. As we meet James, Matt, and Rick, you may be reminded of some children you know.

JAMES

James was a happy little boy. From the time he was born through his seventh year, he didn't seem to have any unusual problems. He walked when he was supposed to, and talked at the right time. He was easy to potty train. To all appearances, he was an average child.

What no one realized was that he was memorizing everything just to get through each school day. James' mother, Emily, is a very perceptive person who knew something was wrong, but she couldn't find anyone who could tell her what it was. Everybody just said, "Boys will be boys."

Toward the end of second grade, James became more difficult to manage. He often accused Emily of not really loving him, and he argued with her constantly. She never felt she was communicating with him in a comfortable, maternal way.

In third grade, James began having academic problems, as the subject matter grew more abstract. He was still trying to memorize everything, but he just couldn't any more, and his grades started to slip. In desperation, he put more and more energy into his lessons, since he really wanted to do well. And, for about a month, he did, until he became so exhausted with the high energy output that he couldn't keep it up any longer. Then his grades went down again and he panicked and also became depressed.

As James' concentration power waned, he had trouble remembering simple tasks. He also became a behavior problem at school and at home. He even started having little quirky body movements, but these were well enough hidden in an active child that no one recognized what they were. He told Emily that he wanted to let his hair grow longer. His reason for this was that he could flip his hair away from his eyes and conceal the nervous movements. Also, he started shuffling his feet, making clicking noises with his heels. As you might guess, James barely made it through the third grade.

As fourth grade began, he had even more trouble keeping up, and his behavior worsened—he was more defiant and harder to manage. When he started having temper tantrums, his parents brought him to see me.

After evaluating James, we realized that he was a depressed child with very low self-esteem. He unconsciously felt that no one cared about him. Also, he was filled with pent-up anger, especially toward authority figures. Passive aggression was exhibiting itself in misbehavior toward the primary authority in his life—his parents, and also toward his teachers.

We discovered three reasons why James was having such trouble in school. First, he had *perceptual problems*. The information coming into his mind was processed in a distorted fashion, and this made the material seem confusing to him. Second, he was *depressed*, and depression can intensify or create a learning problem because concentration is more difficult. Third, he was behaving *passively-aggressively*, getting back at authority by purposely, but unconsciously, making poor grades. However, he was not aware that this was his purpose.

By the time I saw him, James was doing poorly in every part of his life. His learning difficulties had developed into a total life problem. Also, his anti-authority attitude was out of hand. Even at his young age, he was against everything his parents stood for, including spirituality. He hated church and Sunday School, and was a constant disruption in his class.

We began treating James for depression and counseled his parents to deal with his anger by encouraging him to get it out from inside where it was destroying him. After taking these steps, we sought the academic help he needed.

After several months of therapy, James was much improved, and was able to be an affectionate child to his parents, receiving the love they so much wanted to give to him. Displays of affection were pleasant to him now, and he could really believe that his parents meant what they said and did, because he was beginning to develop a positive self-image.

We involved an educational therapist in James' treatment to deal with the passive-aggressive, anti-learning attitude that had grown inside of him. She first worked to create a personal relationship with James. Then, she built on this bond to develop a more positive attitude toward school. She also enrolled him in the special education programs he needed, and helped his teachers understand how to make James feel good about himself and about learning.

As his anger subsided and his depression lifted, James became less passive-aggressive and anti-authority. For the first time, he was receptive to spiritual teaching.

James is fortunate to have such a perceptive mother who wouldn't take a "Boys will be boys" answer to his problems. Both Emily and her husband have made a sincere effort to work with me and the educational therapist to give James a better chance in life. With patience and time, and by example in their home, they will be able to help him develop into a well-rounded adult who will want to follow their spiritual values.

CHILDREN WITH PERCEPTUAL HANDICAPS

In addition to coping with most of the same problems other children have, youngsters with perceptual handicaps must also deal with their own particular difficulties.

Because life is increasingly hard for them, they tend to be anti-authority in every way. As they grow older, they are prone to wrongdoing, even criminal acts. A recent study shows that adolescent males with diagnosed perceptual handicaps are more likely to be involved in juvenile delinquency. In fact, the odds of being judged delinquent are 220 percent greater for them than for their nonhandicapped peers!

Children with perceptual problems are usually depressed, and depression is the one thing we desperately want to avoid in all children and teenagers. The more depressed a child is, the more angry he becomes. Depression produces anger and angry children are much more likely to be passive-aggressive.

When we take an already depressed, passive-aggressive, handicapped child, and superimpose the "normal" depression and passive-aggressive behavior of adolescence, we have a kid who is profoundly depressed and profoundly passive-aggressive.

Long before we can teach values to this child, we have to help him through his anger and depression. We need to let him know that we love him unconditionally and are trying to understand his particular problem. Only then are we on the road to involving him in genuine relationships, including the ultimate relationship, with Jesus Christ.

ADD AND ADHD

In recent years, our educational system has become more adept at identifying children with perceptual problems. The terms Attention Deficit Disorder, ADD, and Attention Deficit Hyperactive Disorder, ADHD, have become well known and popularized. These conditions are highly complex, but many lay people have gained significant understanding about helping such children. As you read, you may wish to refer to the graph at the end of this chapter.

I want to consider ADD and ADHD together, since they have so many similarities. Children in both categories employ inappropriate and destructive ways of handling their anger. They also both involve two neurological problems—

perceptual difficulties and short attention span. ADHD adds the element of hyperactivity, but I am assuming that hyperactivity and short attention span are so closely related that we can discuss them together.

A child with a *short attention span* cannot focus or concentrate long enough to learn well. His attention shifts from one distraction to another and he appears to be restless, careless, and clumsy—hyperactive.

A child with ADHD has real problems focusing on the parent. This makes it difficult for the parent to maintain the child's attention long enough to transmit positive feelings of love. Also, the parent is forced to focus primarily on the child's problems and is repeatedly drawn into the trap of expressing negative feelings to the child.

The vicious cycle continues, the child harboring anger toward the parent because he feels unloved and unaccepted, and the parent in frustration dumping anger on the child. Also, the child is angry at himself for "failing." His growing depression increases the rage within him.

I dislike giving medications to children, but sometimes they are the wise and humane way to go. The medication Ritalin (Methylphenidate) is often appropriate for children with ADHD, so that the child's attention span can be brought to normal and the child can focus on the parents' love. I have seen countless children who for the first time were able to accept their parents' love after taking Ritalin. Of course, the most important factor in keeping the child's emotional tank full is the parents' unconditional love shown with eye contact, physical contact, and focused attention. But if the child has problems receiving that love because of a short attention span, Ritalin or other medications may help.

The other neurological factor in ADHD is *perceptual.*

In one or more of the five senses, and especially in sight and hearing, the child misperceives and misunderstands what she hears or sees. A common perceptual problem is *reversal* or seeing the mirror image of a letter or word. The child may see *was* instead of *saw*, or a *b* instead of a *d*. This condition can cause a reading difficulty called *dyslexia*.

A child with perceptual problems will also have a hard time in accurate reception of feelings from others, and will tend to receive feelings in a negative way. This is the reason a perceptually handicapped child will feel that her parents and other authority figures do not care about her. Of course, in most cases, they truly do, but the child doesn't feel it and so is angry and depressed.

Children with ADHD are extremely prone to childhood and adolescent *depression*. This is difficult to identify because it is not as apparent as in adults. It usually begins when the child is seven or eight years old and deepens to the point that it presents significant problems in the fourth grade.

Childhood depression causes decreased attention span which, of course, worsens the short attention span already present. Therefore, childhood depression decreases the child's ability to concentrate, to remember, and to think or reason clearly. It also causes great amounts of anger which can lead to passive-aggressive attitudes and behavior.

Adolescent depression is usually severe and is revealed in a variety of difficulties. Fortunately, medical people have made good progress in identifying and treating depression in both children and teenagers. Like many other doctors, I will prescribe two types of medication for such children — one to lengthen the attention span, as I mentioned earlier, and the other to control depression. I appreciate antidepressants because they are safe, nonaddictive, and work in a "natural" way. By natural, I mean that they not only make the child feel good, but also correct the biochemical imbalance caused by the depression—the concentration of three hormones, norepinephrine, dopamine, and serotonin. I have seen antidepressants bring children and teenagers out of depression when nothing else could help.

Unfortunately, many people think that a perceptually handicapped child is lazy or stubborn or just plain "dumb." They fail to understand that the child does not perceive or take information from his environment as the average child does. His understanding of the world is distorted.

Imagine the child's dilemma. He is angry because he cannot understand his schoolwork and because his parents nag him for not doing it. Therefore, he doesn't feel understood by his parents. Also, he doesn't get along well with his peers and so feels isolated. By the time he reaches adolescence, he suffers from severe behavioral and emotional disorders.

MATT

One afternoon some years ago, I attended my son Dale's baseball game. I recognized Matt, a member of the opposing team, since he and his parents had been to see me earlier that year. At thirteen, he was perceptually handicapped and the neighborhood nuisance.

I found a seat next to Larry, Matt's adult neighbor, just as Matt was coming up to bat.

"Hey, Larry," Matt called, "which side of the base is the right side? I think I bat righthanded. The kid who just batted is left-handed. Should I stand where he did?"

"No, Matt," Larry answered impatiently. "You should stand on the other side of the plate."

Larry turned to me, "Isn't that the dumbest thing? Matt doesn't know the right side from the left side of home plate."

"Maybe he has some learning problems," I offered.

"He sure does! If he wasn't so blamed ornery, he could learn something."

"No, really, Larry," I continued, "there are people who don't know left from right."

"That's impossible. There's nothing wrong with him that a little willow switch now and then wouldn't cure!"

Poor Matt! Besides the normal anxieties of competing, he has the added frustration of perceptual difficulties and a not very understanding neighbor. Fortunately, his parents and school have recognized his problems and are helping him.

It is critical that parents of children like Matt fill their kids' emotional tanks daily. Perceptually handicapped children have great difficulty understanding positive feelings for them. For this reason, they need extra helpings of love, physical contact, and focused attention from the important people in their lives.

To convey love, we use eye contact which involves visual perception; physical contact which is an overwhelmingly complex sense; and focused attention which requires seeing, hearing, and the possession of a certain degree of logic. If a perceptual problem exists in any of these areas, the child's understanding is distorted, thus creating great frustration for both the child and adult seeking to communicate with him.

It is not only the child who experiences great pain, for his parents run the whole gamut of emotions before they can come to grips with the fact that their child is suffering from perceptual problems. They may begin by denying that the problem exists. Then they take the child for second and third opinions. They also isolate themselves, thinking that no one understands them.

Next, they begin on a guilt trip, sure that they caused the problem. They question their childrearing: "Were we too strict? Were we too easygoing?" Then comes the anger: "We're surely not the guilty persons in this situation. We've done everything we can. It must be the doctor who doesn't know what he is talking about. And the school—they don't know how to educate properly!"

Finally, the parents start blaming each other. When the child sees this, he feels afraid and even more depressed. At this point, parents who really want to help their child will commit themselves to counseling. There they will find hope as well as specific information on how to deal with their child's problem. Once they have hope, they alleviate the child's depression and anger.

RICK

Rick, a handsome, dark-eyed, ten-year-old walked into my office well ahead of his mother, Joyce.

"I sure hope you can find out what is wrong, Dr. Campbell," he said, "because my mother worries a lot about me. Sometimes she even cries. I hate to see her do that. Maybe you can tell her something today that will make her feel better." What a great kid!

Joyce was a single parent. Her husband left a year ago, just about the time Rick's problem began to surface at school. She was a sincere mother who tried to do everything she could for Rick.

His teacher had told Joyce that there wasn't anything wrong with Rick except an excess of maternal attention! "You're trying too hard to compensate for the absence of his father, and you're spoiling him. He can read. He is just being stubborn to get all the attention he can," the teacher stated firmly.

And so, armed with this opinion, Joyce gave Rick less attention, but tutored him every night after school. Nothing worked. His behavior problems increased, and his grades dropped to failing. This was when Joyce brought him to me.

After we evaluated him, I called Rick and his mother into my office. I said, "Well, Rick, we'll just see what we can do to make your mother and you feel better."

I went over the tests with them, and showed them that Rick had a visual perceptual problem and a slight attention deficit. "But don't worry, you're a bright boy, Rick. And I doubt that you are too stubborn to try to read. I think you are all right and I'm going to try to help you."

Rick's eyes lit up. "Listen to that, Mom. I'm not dumb after all. You don't have to worry so much about me now."

Rick was feeling very responsible for his mother's unhappiness. After beginning treatment, Rick was able to get rid of some of the guilt which had caused him to feel even more depressed.

FAMOUS ADHD PEOPLE

When working with ADHD children, I love to tell them and their parents about well-known persons who had the problem. I emphasize my belief that ADHD and ADD are misnamed, that these children do not have a "disorder." They are normal children who were born about 150 years too late and so have to go to schools that offer a kind of learning that is hard for perceptually handicapped people.

When school attendance was not universally mandated, people with perceptual problems could learn in their own ways. I am something of a history buff, and several years ago I noticed that many of our outstanding forebears had perceptual problems. My favorite is Kit Carson. Being raised in New Mexico, I was fascinated with the way he excelled in almost every aspect of frontier life in the 1800s. Not only was he involved in most of the significant happenings in the Southwest, but he had a good heart and truly cared for Native Americans. He was well loved by the Spanish Americans and respected by the political leaders of his day.

Several people wrote biographies of Kit Carson, and finally he wrote his autobiography. I had trouble finding this last work because it was not highly regarded. When I finally did secure a copy, I began to realize that Carson had ADHD. When I visited the Kit Carson Museum in Taos, I was spellbound as I read his notes and letters and came to understand why his autobiography was one of his few failures. His penmanship and writing style were typical of many ADHD persons I have known.

One of my favorite contemporary persons is O.D. McKee who founded McKee Bakeries of Collegedale, Tennessee, the producer of Little Debbie Snack Cakes. What an inspiring story!

I love to tell children with ADHD and their parents that almost every person with ADHD has some special gift or talent. Sadly, these talents are not always allowed to blossom because of the problems we have already discussed. These families need to know that there is a special strength in these children. Their unique gifts will be discovered and allowed to grow only if the parents understand how to train the children to manage their anger appropriately. Only then can the defiant, anti-authority resistance of passive-aggressive behavior be prevented. It is almost always this type of anger that keeps the children from discovering and using their gifts—which are usually mechanical in nature, but can bloom in every area.

Finally, I love to tell these wonderful children and their parents that *everyone* has perceptual problems. No one is perceptually perfect. You know the result if ten people each tell you their version of an accident. Or you may remember that simple childhood whispering game, where one person tells the one next to him a message that is then passed along the line until the last person reveals what he or she heard.

The problems of most perceptually handicapped children can be minimized if they are caught early enough. James and Rick are fortunate because their parents discovered their problems in time. Catching the problem "in time" means before the child reaches adolescence.

When it remains untreated into adolescence, the child usually experiences much more than academic difficulty. He often has experimented with drugs, sex, stealing, running away, and may even have attempted suicide.

I have told the stories of James, Matt, and Rick so that you might better understand the dilemmas of perceptually handicapped children. Helping these learning-disabled children develop into wholeness takes time, patience, and understanding, but it is well worth the effort.

LINDA—A CHRONICALLY ILL CHILD

Perceptual deficits are not the only special problems that affect the behavior of children. Chronic physical ailments can also create emotional and behavioral controversy. We can become so involved in the daily needs of chronically ill children that we overlook their emotional needs.

As physically impaired children grow older, they become increasingly bitter about their disease or handicap. They also feel angry at their caring parents, because the parents have inadvertently replaced the natural giving of love with daily medical attention. These children can turn defiant, not only toward their parents but toward all authority.

Linda's mother described her as "a fussy baby from the very beginning. We tried everything we could think of, but we just couldn't seem to make her happy. When she was three, the pediatrician discovered a chronic heart defect. Since then, our life with her has been one trip after another to specialists."

"How is her physical health now?" I asked.

"It is stabilized," her father answered, "but her pregnancy certainly won't help her any."

"I see you have another child, a son," I noted, as I scanned their file. "How is his health?"

"Oh, it's perfect," Linda's mother answered. "We're so proud of Jeff. He's a fine athlete and an accomplished pianist."

"Has Linda ever developed any hobbies?"

"No," her father answered. "We've been so busy attending to her health problems that we never had the time to do much else with her. Don't get me wrong. It's not that we didn't want to. She has always been such a cranky kid that we never could talk her into doing anything other than going to school. And now, here she is pregnant. I guess it's too late."

"At least she is going to marry the father of the baby next week," his wife added. "Maybe that will make her happy. We have done all we know to do, Dr. Campbell, but we surely went wrong somewhere. She has been very depressed lately. I'm relieved that we talked her into coming to see you. I sure hope you can get through to her. She's in a sorry frame of mind to start a marriage."

"Why don't both of you wait outside, and let me talk with Linda," I suggested.

Curled up in a chair in the corner of the waiting room was Linda—seventeen years old and pregnant.

"Would you like to come in, Linda?" I asked, as I walked over to her.

"Why not? That's what they brought me here for." As she sat down in a chair in my office, she said with a frown, "I don't know what good my being here is going to do. You can't change things."

"You're right, Linda. I can't change things, but maybe in time I can help you to change the way you feel about things."

When Linda began to open up, my suspicions were confirmed. She was a classic example of the chronically ill child whose parents spent so much time caring for her physical needs that they forgot about her emotional needs.

" 'Jeff can do this—Jeff can do that!' That's all I ever heard. 'Let's go to Jeff's game, Linda. It'll do you good to get out of the house. Let's go to Jeff's piano recital, Linda. Maybe you'll decide to start taking piano lessons.' And you should see the grades Jeff makes—straight A's. I made C's and I think that is plenty good enough."

I've just begun counseling with Linda, but I feel that she can be helped with her depression. I know that her parents love her and didn't realize that they substituted medical attention for emotional attention. Linda's low grades and her pregnancy were both subconscious acts of defiance against this seeming indifference.

THREE PITFALLS

In my years of treating chronically ill and perceptually handicapped children, I have discovered that there are three principal pitfalls for parents. The first is the one illustrated by Linda's case — substituting medical attention for emotional fulfillment.

The second pitfall is a lack of behavioral control and firmness. These parents often feel such pity, and sometimes even blame and guilt, that they do not try to provide normal control for the child's behavior. This results in a manipulative child who uses illness to control the parents.

The third pitfall is failure to train these children to manage anger. Handicapped children are generally more difficult to teach because they tend toward anti-authority attitudes. Their parents are then caught between pity and guilt, on the one hand, and their own anger, on the other.

Everything we have discussed in this book certainly applies to these precious children. But their parents have little room for error. It is so easy for them to fall into the vicious cycle of rage and guilt. It is critical for these parents to understand the possible pitfalls as early as possible. The longer a difficult situation continues, the more difficult it will be to correct, especially when it involves anti-authority attitudes.

Yet, as we have seen, success can come to the handicapped child if the problem is detected and help is obtained in time. If you have a special problem child in your family, I hope that you are finding appropriate professional help and also that you are providing the unconditional love that will keep your child's emotional tank full.

I have seen innumerable children with special problems who have done beautifully. For most of these dear ones, their handicaps have become challenges which have helped to mold their character in wonderful ways.

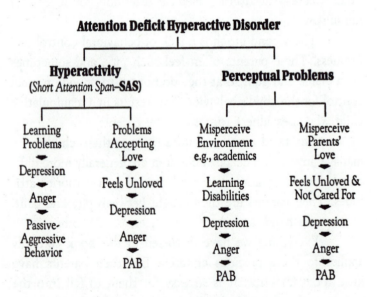

A Final Word to Parents

It is a difficult world you are preparing your children to enter. But now you have some key information that they and you need. When you teach your children how to manage anger, you're giving them a strong advantage for the future. It is something like giving them a compass so that they can avoid life's most devastating problems, stay on the positive side, and more ably reach for fulfillment.

As a last word of encouragement, I would like to share something with you that will help you put your parenting in perspective.

Some parents are so *overly conscientious* that they almost worry themselves to death. They tend to think that there is such a thing as being "the perfect parent." They're afraid that if they make even one mistake, their children will turn out terribly. This fear paralyzes them, making their parenting more difficult and less effective.

Other parents tend to be *authoritarian*, "captains of the ship." They issue commands and relate to their children as if they were military recruits. This type of parenting may seem to work well with some children, but in time they become progressively resentful and anti-authority in their attitudes.

Some of us vacillate between these two types of parenting. Yet, regardless of what type of parents we are, what matters most is to come to the place where we can relax and enjoy our children. Few parents do this naturally. One of the most wonderful happenings in my own parenting occurred when I learned to truly relax with my children and genuinely enjoy them—at any age.

Although parenting is a difficult and often perplexing responsibility, it can be understood as our means of meeting the needs of our children. Any conscientious parent can be taught how to do this, regardless of their personality. The main requirement is willingness and desire.

Since you are reading this book, you certainly qualify. As simple as this sounds, most parents have a deep fear of not being good enough, primarily because they don't know what is necessary to actually be good parents. And yet, if they are constantly uncertain, parenting will seem an overwhelming responsibility. Perhaps I can best illustrate this by telling you a story.

June, a forty-five-year-old mother of three, sought my advice about her elderly mother. June is conscientious and goodhearted. She had a close relationship with her mother until the last two years, when her mother became increasingly difficult. She criticized June for everything and became more and more demanding, complaining that June did not visit or call often enough. Eventually, June was spending so much time trying to care for her mother's needs that she was neglecting her own family. She had tried every tactic she could think of, including a frank discussion with her mother, but nothing had any effect on her mother's unreasonable demands.

I told June, "You are being a good daughter."

She replied, "How could I be when my mother is so disappointed in me all the time?"

I then asked her, "Have you considered what the requirements are for being a good daughter in your situation?"

June answered, "No, I've never thought about that."

I asked her to make a list of what she thought would make her a good daughter. She naturally assumed she would have a long list.

When June and I talked again, she said how amazed she was that she had only six items on her list—things like visiting her mother once a week and calling twice a week, sending gifts and cards for birthday and Christmas, etc. When June saw that she not only met the requirements but in many ways exceeded them, she felt better about herself, instead of confused and downhearted as she had before

June's next challenge was to learn to be relaxed, upbeat, and pleasant, as well as firm with her mother, regardless of her mother's mood or attitude. June was able to do this because she *knew* she was being a good daughter.

I then asked June to make another list, but this time about her parenting. Of course, this role is much more complex than her role as a grown daughter, but the same rules apply. June determined the basic requirements of being a good parent and then made her list. She reviewed the list about once a week to keep it up to date for each child.

This had the same freeing experience with her children as with her mother. Now that she knew she was a good mother, she could be relaxed, upbeat, pleasant, and yet firm with her children. Best of all, June found herself enjoying each of them and appreciating their unique features more.

I urge you to follow June's example. You might use this book as a guide and make your own list. This will encourage you to reread this book as your children grow up. And be sure that you update your list as June did, to keep pace with your growing children.

God bless you!

Notes

Chapter One
1. Neil Clark Warren, *Making Anger Your Ally* (Colorado Springs: Focus on the Family Publishing, 1990), 77, 55.

2. Ibid., 121.

3. Ibid., 97.

Chapter Two
1. Thomas Sowell, "Who Says It's Hopeless?" *Reader's Digest*, June 1994, 180.

2. Benjamin Spock, *A Better World for Our Children* (Bethesda: National Press Books, 1994).

3. Neil Clark Warren, *Making Anger Your Ally* (Colorado Springs: Focus on the Family Publishing, 1990), 8.

Chapter Three
1. "Burdened Teens Feel Estranged from Adults," *The Chattanooga Times*, 14 July 1994.

2. Stuart Goldman, "Murder as Therapy," *National Review*, 45, 29 November 1993, 44–46.

Chapter Four
1. Adapted from *How to Really Love Your Child* (Wheaton, Ill.: Victor Books, 1977), chapter 3.

2. David Seamands, *Healing for Damaged Emotions* (Wheaton, Ill.: Victor Books, 1981), 61.

3. Ibid., 63–64.

4. David Seamands, *Putting Away Childish Things* (Wheaton, Ill.: Victor Books, 1982), 33.

5. Neil Clark Warren, *Making Anger Your Ally* (Colorado Springs: Focus on the Family Publishing, 1990), 123.

6. Ibid., 123–24.

7. Ibid., 125.

Chapter Five
1. Andrew D. Lester, *Coping with Anger: A Christian Guide* (Philadelphia: The Westminster Press, 1983), 34–35.

2. Carol Tavris, *Anger: The Misunderstood Emotion* (New York: Simon and Schuster, 1989), 47.

3. "The Traits of Wrath in Men and Women," *USA Today*, 11 August 1994.

4. Meg Eastman, *Taming the Dragon in Your Child* (New York: John Wiley and Sons, 1994), 4.

Chapter Six
1. Ruth N. Koch and Kenneth C. Haugk, *Speaking the Truth in Love: Now to Be an Assertive Christian* (St. Louis: Stephen Ministries, 1992), 16–17, 19.

2. Ibid., 22.

Chapter Seven
1. Leonard D. Eron, *Reason to Hope: A Psycho-Social Perspective on Violence and Youth* (Washington, D.C.: American Psychological Association), December 1994.

2. Meg Eastman, *Taming the Dragon in Your Child* (New York: John Wiley and Sons, 1994), 187–88.

3. Andrew D. Lester, *Coping with Your Anger* (Philadelphia: The Westminster Press, 1983), 59.

4. Howard S. Friedman and Stephanie Booth-Kersley, "The Disease-Prone Personality: A Meta-Analytic View of the Construct," *American Psychologist* 42, 1987, 539–55.

5. Carol Tavris, *Anger: The Misunderstood Emotion* (New York: Simon and Schuster, 1989), 129.

6. Ibid., 131–42.

7. Ibid., 137.

8. Ibid., 139–41.

9. Ibid., 146.

Chapter Nine
1. Ellen Goodman, "A Mom Fights Media Madness," *Family Circle*, 14 March 1995, 134.

2. Gladys Hunt, *Honey for a Child's Heart* (Grand Rapids: Zondervan Publishing House, 1989)

3. William Kilpatrick and Gregory and Suzanne M. Wolfe, *Books That Build Character: A Guide to Teaching Your Child Moral Values through Stories* (New York: Simon and Schuster, Inc., 1994).

4. William Bennett, *The Book of Virtues: A Treasury of Great Moral Stories* (New York: Simon and Schuster, Inc., 1993).

5. Martin E. Seligman, *Learned Optimism* (New York: Simon and Schuster, Inc., 1980).

6. Thomas Gordon, *Parent Effectiveness Training* (New York: David McKay, Inc., 1970).

7. Meg Eastman, *Taming the Dragon in Your Child* (New York: John Wiley and Sons, 1994).

Chapter Eleven
1. H.B. London, Jr. and Neil B. Wiseman, *Pastors at Risk* (Wheaton, Ill.: Victor, 1993), 22.

2. Ibid., 29.

Chapter Twelve
1. C.A. Oliphant, *Sweet Success* (Cleveland, Tenn.: Sundial Press, 1994).